RISE AND THRIVE

A Woman's Guide to Unlocking Her Inner Strength and True Potential

JUDY DYER

RISE AND THRIVE:
A Woman's Guide to Unlocking Her
Inner Strength and True Potential
by Judy Dyer

ISBN: 979-8337807027

ALSO BY JUDY DYER

Empath: A Complete Guide for Developing Your Gift and Finding Your Sense of Self

The Highly Sensitive: How to Stop Emotional Overload, Relieve Anxiety, and Eliminate Negative Energy

The Empowered Empath: A Simple Guide on Setting Boundaries, Controlling Your Emotions, and Making Life Easier

The Power of Emotions: How to Manage Your Feelings and Overcome Negativity

Borderline Personality Disorder: A Complete BPD Guide for Managing Your Emotions and Improving Your Relationships

CONTENTS

INTRODUCTION

Have you ever stopped to ask yourself what you truly desire outside of the expectations and roles enforced on you by society? Have you ever considered what your ideal life would look like where you feel fulfilled, completely empowered, and balanced? Many of you reading this will answer no to these questions because it's not the norm for women to consider what they truly want out of life. It's the norm to conform to society's expectations of you, and if you don't, you risk being labeled a rebel.

Why do I say this? Because this is what I experienced when I began to challenge my conditioning. Let me explain.

Growing up, I don't ever remember having a conversation with my parents about the purpose of life. But I do remember my mother buying me dolls and kitchen sets and reminding me that the most important thing I will ever do as a woman is get married and have children. She truly believed this because that was all she knew. My mother was a housewife with no education and no skills useful for the workforce, so she could only teach me what she knew.

When I got together with my female friends, their main concern was finding a boyfriend. All of our conversations centered around finding our knight in shining armor, having our dream wedding and starting a family. My friends reinforced what my mom taught me and so did society. The messages were clear: Women were expected to get married and have children, and if they didn't, they were ostracized.

When I decided to go to college, my mother's main concern was whether there were any potential candidates for marriage because she wanted grandchildren. Although I didn't really know what I wanted to do with my life at the time, I knew I wanted more than what my mother was pushing on me.

Fast-forward ten years—I had a master's degree in public administration and was working as a bookkeeper for a very prestigious law firm, but I hated my job. The money was good, I owned my home, drove a nice car, and I was in a steady relationship. But there was something missing. While my single female friends were obsessing over their biological clocks, that was the last thing on my mind. Also, I paid attention to my childhood friends who were married with children; many of them were terribly unhappy because they had goals and aspirations they couldn't reach due to the demands of family life. Deep down, I knew there was more to life than the one I was living. I admired passionate people who knew exactly what they wanted, set goals for themselves and achieved them. I wanted what they had but I didn't know how to get it. Evidently, it was possible because people were doing it, so I decided to learn everything I could about how to create the life that you want. I applied what I had learned, and here I am today—a number one bestselling author living the life of my dreams.

I wrote this book because there are too many women in the world not fulfilling their potential. They've got so much to give, but they are stuck in a place of stagnation because no one ever taught them that it is possible to break free from the shackles of societal expectations. Doing what your heart desires takes courage. That's why many people put their dreams on the shelf and leave them there. But I want to teach you how to shift your mindset so you can brush the dust off those dreams and bring them to life again. In this book you will learn:

- How to develop inner strength to empower you to become successful

- How to develop a resilient mindset so you can crush the goals you set for yourself

- How to become the most confident version of yourself

- Tools to help you find your purpose and live a meaningful life

- How to identify toxic relationships in your life and leave them

- Tips on how to find your voice and speak your truth

Ladies, listen—you are about to embark on a journey that is going to transform the entire trajectory of your life. There is no looking back now. The old has passed. You are entering a new season that is going to absolutely blow your mind! If you're ready to get started, keep reading...

Oh, and by the way, while I wrote this book for all women, I reference empaths and highly sensitive people quite a bit because I am an empath but I also have a lot of highly sensitive traits. If this doesn't apply to you, let it fly.

I wish you every success on your journey to living your best life!

JOIN OUR FACEBOOK GROUP

In order to maximize the value you receive from this book, I highly encourage you to join our tight-knit community on Facebook. Here we focus on mastering your gifts as an Empath, but you will be able to connect and share with other like-minded readers to continue your growth.

Taking this journey alone is not recommended, and this can be an excellent support network for you.

It would be great to connect with you there,

Judy Dyer

To Join, Visit:
www.pristinepublish.com/empathgroup

Or Scan the QR Code on Your Phone:

DOWNLOAD THE AUDIO VERSION OF THIS BOOK FOR FREE

If you love listening to audiobooks on the go or would enjoy a narration as you read along, I have great news for you. You can download the audiobook version of *Rise and Thrive* for FREE just by signing up for a FREE 30-day Audible trial!

Visit: www.pristinepublish.com/audiobooks

Or Scan the QR Code on Your Phone:

YOUR FREE GIFT—HEYOKA EMPATH

A lot of empaths feel trapped, as if they've hit a glass ceiling they can't penetrate. They know there's another level to their gift, but they can't seem to figure out what it is. They've read dozens of books, been to counseling, and confided in other experienced empaths, but that glass ceiling remains. They feel alone and alienated from the rest of the world. They know they've got so much more to give, but they can't access it. Does this sound like you?

The inability to connect to your true and authentic self is a tragedy. Being robbed of the joy of embracing the full extent of your humanity is a terrible misfortune. The driving force of human nature is to live according to one's own sense of self, values, and emotions. Since the beginning of time, philosophers, writers, and scholars have argued that authenticity is one of the most important elements of an individual's well-being.

When there's a disconnect between a person's inner being and their expressions, it can be psychologically damaging. Heyokas are the most powerful type of empaths, and many of them are not fully aware of who they are. While other empaths experience feelings of overwhelm and exhaustion from absorbing others' energy and emotions, heyoka empaths experience an additional aspect of exhaustion in that they are fighting a constant battle with their inability to be completely authentic.

The good news is that the only thing stopping you from becoming your authentic self is a lack of knowledge. You need to know exactly who you are so you can tap into the resources that have been lying dormant within you. In this bonus e-book, you'll gain in-depth information about the seven signs that you're a heyoka empath, and why certain related abilities are such powerful traits. You'll find many of the answers to the questions you've been searching for your entire life, such as:

- Why you feel uncomfortable when you're around certain people

- How you always seem to find yourself on the right path even though your decisions are not based on logic or rationale

- The reason you get so offended when you find out others have lied to you

- Why you analyze everything in such detail

- The reason humor is such an important part of your life

- Why you refuse to follow the crowd, regardless of the consequences

- The reason strangers and animals are drawn to you

There are three main components to authenticity: understanding who you are; expressing who you are; and letting the world experience who you are. Your first step on this journey is to know who you are, and with these seven signs that you're a heyoka empath, you'll find out. I've included snippets about the first three signs in this description to give you full confidence that you're on the right track:

Sign 1: You Feel and Understand Energy

Heyoka empaths possess a natural ability to tap into energy. They can walk into a room and immediately discern the atmosphere. When an individual walks past them, they can literally see into their soul because they can sense the aura that person is carrying. But empaths also understand their own energy, and they allow it to guide them. You will often hear this ability referred to as "the sixth sense." The general consensus is that only a few people have this gift. But the reality is that everyone was born with the ability to feel energy; it's just been demonized and turned into something spooky, when in actual fact it's the most natural state to operate in.

Sign 2: You Are Led by Your Intuition

Do you find that you just know things? You don't spend hours, days, and weeks agonizing over decisions—you can just feel that something is the right thing to do, and you go ahead and do it. That's because you're led by your intuition and you're connected to the deepest part of yourself. You know your soul, you listen to it, and you trust it. People like Oprah Winfrey, Steve Jobs, and Richard Branson followed their intuition steadfastly, and it led them to become some of the most successful people in the history of the world. Living from within is the way we were created to be, and those who trust this ability will find their footing in life a lot more quickly than others do. Think of it as a GPS system; when it's been programmed properly, it will always take you to your destination via the fastest route.

Sign 3: You Believe in Complete Honesty

In general, empaths don't like being around negative energy, and there's nothing that can shift a positive frequency faster than dishonesty. Anything that isn't the truth is a lie, even the tiny ones that we excuse away as "white lies." And as soon as they're released from someone's mouth, so is negative energy. Living an authentic life requires complete honesty at all times, and although the truth may hurt, it's better than not being able to trust someone. Heyoka empaths get very uncomfortable in the presence of liars. They are fully aware that the vibrations of the person don't match the words they are saying. Have you ever experienced a brain freeze mid-conversation? All of a sudden you just couldn't think straight, you couldn't articulate yourself properly, and things just got really awkward? That's because your empath antenna picked up on a lie.

Heyoka Empath: 7 Signs You're A Heyoka Empath & Why It's So Powerful is a revolutionary tool that will help you transition from uncertainty to complete confidence in who you are. In this easy-to-read guide, I will walk you through exactly what makes you a heyoka empath. I've done the research for you, so no more spending hours, days, weeks, and even years searching for answers, because everything you need is right here in this book.

You have a deep need to share yourself with the world, but you've been too afraid because you knew something was missing. The information within the pages of this book is the missing piece in the jigsaw puzzle of your life. There's no turning back now!

Get *Heyoka Empath* for Free by Visiting

www.pristinepublish.com/empathbonus

Or Scan the QR Code on Your Phone:

CHAPTER 1:

YOUR STRENGTH COMES FROM WITHIN

What do all the most successful people in the world have in common? It's not money, power, or fame—it's inner strength. Becoming the person you were destined to be requires an extreme amount of resilience and grit because you are going against the grain. I am no conspiracy theorist; however, I do find it mighty strange that we live in a society that dictates how we ought to live. Go to school, get an education, get a job, work for forty years as you struggle to pay bills, and then die! Not to be morbid, but that is a very depressing existence, yet billions of people live this way because that is how the world has told them they are supposed to live and so they don't know any other way. It takes an exceptionally strong person to break out of this mold and refuse to conform to the norms and values of society. Your family and friends will reject you; they won't believe in your dreams. Whether directly or indirectly, they will tell you you're delusional and attempt to keep you at the bottom of the mountain with them. This is not intentional, by the way—they simply can't see how you are going to escape your reality, because as far as they are concerned, success isn't for people like them, so how dare you think you can become someone other than who they perceive you to be? If you are going to break free from the constraints of societal expectations, you must develop inner strength. Let's start by defining the term *inner strength*.

What Is Inner Strength?

Inner strength is a profound, resolute belief in yourself. It is not defined by your circumstances, the opinions of others, or anything external. Inner strength is solely defined by how you feel about yourself.

It's all well and good having a theoretical understanding of inner strength—but what does it look like in practice? At the beginning of the chapter, I mentioned that all successful people have inner strength in common. Let's take a look at how some of them became who they are today.

Jim Carrey: Despite being raised in poverty and having a childhood devoid of joy and happiness, Jim Carrey overcame the odds and became one of the most successful comedic actors in history. His family was so poor that he dropped out of school at fifteen and found a job as a janitor to help support his family. Due to his many struggles, Carrey comforted himself by making funny faces at himself in the mirror. He would lock himself in his room and do this for hours. It was during these moments of solitude that Jim Carrey decided he was going to become a famous comedian. He was so serious that at the age of ten, he submitted his résumé to *The Carol Burnett Show*. Despite doing everything he could to make ends meet, the family were unable to pay the mortgage, and the Carreys lost their home.

Carrey landed his first stand-up gig at Yuk Yuk's Comedy Club in Toronto, but the audience didn't like his act and he was booed off the stage. But he continued practicing, and by 1979, he was making a full-time living out of his performances. His name became known amongst famous comedians and he became the opening act for many of them. During this time, *Saturday Night Live* was known for giving the next generation of comedians a stage to become successful in Hollywood. Having done extremely well as an independent comedian, Carrey believed he would get a spot on the renowned TV show, but he was rejected three times. Although disappointed, he stopped auditioning for the show and focused on establishing himself as a stand-up comedian. He eventually got his first commercial break on Fox's *In Living Color*, and later went on to play the lead role as the pet detective in the film *Ace Ventura*. His career has spanned over three decades, during which time he has won several awards for his performances. He currently has a net worth of $180 million!

What can we learn from Jim Carrey's sensational journey from poverty to prosperity? Firstly, while he had a difficult upbringing, it was actually preparing him for success. Had Carrey been raised in an affluent family, there is a possibility he may not have discovered his gift. He tapped into his talent out of sheer desperation. He channeled his pain and frustration into mastering his craft—and it paid dividends. He developed resilience from a young age, and it was this resilience that shielded him when he was booed off stage at his first stand-up performance. It was the same resilience that motivated him to continue on his career path after being rejected from *Saturday Night Live* three times. Jim Carrey trusted in his abilities and he refused to allow anyone to dictate his future. I am sure he had many people telling him to give up. That maybe he just wasn't good enough to make it. But he drowned out the noise and listened to the still, small voice within that told him he was born to do this and that he should keep taking destiny steps until his dream turned into a reality.

Steven Spielberg: Steven Spielberg always knew he wanted to become a film director, but one of the first problems he encountered was that he wasn't academically bright. He struggled in school because he was dyslexic, but that wasn't discovered until he was sixty years old. He was relentlessly bullied because he couldn't read properly and neither was he any good at sports. But it was his passion for filmmaking that kept him grounded. At age twelve, Spielberg directed his first film and continued working on several projects over the years. Certain he wanted a career in filmmaking, Spielberg applied to the University of Southern California's School of Cinematic Arts, but, despite his exceptional résumé, was rejected not once, not twice, but three times! Because of his inner strength, he did not let this faze him. He knew he had a gift and he was passionate about it, so instead of allowing those rejections to define him and giving up on his dreams, Spielberg invested in himself and mastered his craft by making short films. His efforts landed him an internship with Universal Studios. His talent spoke for itself, and he gained the attention of the top executives. It wasn't long before he directed his first feature film, *The Sugarland Express*—and the rest is history. Today, Steven Spielberg is one of the most successful film directors of all time, having directed some of the most iconic films of this generation including *Schindler's List*, *Jurassic Park*, *E.T.*, and *Jaws*.

What can we learn from Stephen Spielberg's story? Disability doesn't define you. Being bullied doesn't define you. Rejection doesn't define you. In fact, rejection will redirect you and walk you right into your destiny. I believe in divine timing and divine alignment. You must be at the right place at the right time to walk into the opportunities that have been destined for you. But for this to take place, you must be resilient, because the route you thought you should take is often not the route that will get you to your final destination. Before you arrive at your place of purpose, the doors you wanted to walk through will get shut in your face multiple times. Spielberg didn't apply for the University of Southern California's School of Cinematic Arts once—he applied three times! Why? Because he had his heart set on attending the university. He truly believed that if he was going to make it, he had to go down the traditional route of education. But the universe had other plans. When he realized that he had done all he could do, and that the university was not going to accept him, he moved on to plan B— and that is what ushered him into a realm of success I am certain his mind had not conceived at the time. Spielberg believed in himself, and that was all he needed to become who he is today.

I could write an entire book about people who have succeeded despite the odds, because there are thousands, perhaps millions, of examples. My question to you is *what makes you any different?* Again, Jim Carrey and Steven Spielberg had one thing in common—inner strength. Neither of them were born with a silver spoon in their mouth. They were not nepo babies; their parents didn't have connections in the industry. They knew what they were good at, they developed their craft, and they didn't stop until they made it.

How to Cultivate Inner Strength

The best personal trainers will start by strengthening your core muscles because they know how important they are to how the rest of your body functions. Your core muscles are a group of hip and trunk muscles surrounding the abdomen, spine, viscera, and hip. Whether you are playing basketball, sweeping the floor, putting on your shoes, or lifting a heavy object, the motions used come from your core. Consequently, inflexible or weak core muscles affect the use of your arms and legs, which limits the power of your movements. Do you struggle to run up and down stairs, lift weights, or stand all day while at work? If you have answered yes to any of these questions, you've probably got weak core muscles. Likewise, inner strength is essential to living a full and victorious life. Without it, you will fail.

If your strength doesn't come from within, you will crumble when adversity strikes, you will quit at the first hurdle, and you will depend on external validation to carry you. But when you have inner strength, you keep pushing regardless of your circumstances, you refuse to give up when it appears that there is an unscalable mountain standing between you and your dreams, and you rely on *yourself* for validation. Developing your inner strength is the first chapter because without it, you won't get very far. This life that we are living is not a fairy tale—it's brutal, and it will take everything you've got if you want to live the life you know you deserve. Here are some tips on how to cultivate inner strength:

Study It: I know you are reading a chapter about inner strength, but there is a lot more to it than what I have written in this chapter. You see, no one is born with inner strength; it is a skill you develop over time. As you read this, you have made a conscious decision to build inner strength. As with all skills, with practice, you will master it. But first, you must learn all that you can about it. Here are some books you can read about how to develop inner strength:

- *Can't Hurt Me: Master Your Mind and Defy the Odds* by David Goggins

- *Grit: The Power of Passion and Perseverance* by Angela Duckworth

- *The Hurt Artist: My Journal from Suicidal Junkie to Ironman* by Shane Niemeyer

- *The Way of the Warrior: An Ancient Path to Inner Peace* by Erwin Raphael McManus

- *Life Under Fire: How to Build Inner Strength and Thrive Under Pressure* by Jason Fox

It's important to understand that whatever you read, you must apply. I often hear the quote, "Knowledge is power," but I would like to add to that and say, "Knowledge *with application* is power." There is no point in having access to information that can change your life if you are not going to use it.

Practice Self-Awareness: People struggle with self-awareness because when we don't like something about ourselves, we become defensive and want to protect ourselves, and most people protect themselves through denial. If you are in denial about who you are, and the improvements you need to make, you will never change. Self-awareness is about having an in-depth understanding of who you are and having the ability to step outside of yourself and see yourself as others see you. People who lack self-awareness never admit their mistakes, struggle with constructive criticism, make bad decisions, and have difficulty expressing their emotions. All of which make it difficult for someone to change their behavior. Have you ever met an old person who is stuck in their ways? They have accepted that this is just the way they are and they have no intention of changing, regardless of the negative effect their behavior has on themselves and others.

Self-awareness helps you develop inner strength because it gives you emotional stability. When you are emotionally stable, your emotions don't control you—you control your emotions. This means that when the storms of life hit you, they can't move you. Many people make terrible decisions because they are unable to control their emotions. For example, at the extreme end, we have crimes of passion where a disgruntled lover commits murder because their partner ended the relationship. Then there are people who will do things like eat too much because they are depressed, or go on a shopping spree with their rent money to make themselves feel better. You don't want to fall into either of these categories; therefore, developing self-awareness is essential. Here are some tips on how to become more self-aware:

- **Practice Mindfulness:** Most people spend their mental energy thinking about the past or the future, but rarely do they focus on the here and now unless they have to. For example, while you are washing the dishes, you are thinking about the work you need to do at the office tomorrow. While driving the kids to soccer practice, you are thinking about the meeting you had with your boss last week. Being present helps you connect with your body, mind, and environment. You can practice mindfulness at any time simply by paying attention to your surroundings. For instance, while you are washing the dishes, focus on the process and think about things like what the bubbles feel like on your hands, the sound of the running water, and the smell of the food as you wash it off the dishes. Apply the same technique with all the other activities you participate in—focus on what you are doing at the moment and nothing else.

- **Spend Time Reflecting:** Self-reflection involves examining your thoughts, motivations, feelings, and actions. It helps you gain a deeper understanding of yourself. Self-reflection plays an important role in your personal development and growth because it gives you insight into the habits that are helping you, and the ones that are harming you. Self-reflection requires you to spend time alone and look inwards. It is a good idea to ask yourself questions and write down your answers so you have a clear idea of the improvements you need to make. Here are some questions to ask yourself during your time of self-reflection:

- How can I learn from the recent mistakes I have made?
- What obstacles have I faced and what have I done to overcome them?
- What can I do to step out of my comfort zone?
- What makes me happy?
- What makes me sad?
- What makes me angry?
- What am I passionate about?
- What is holding me back from achieving my dreams?
- What do I want my life to look like ten years from now?
- What are my strengths and weaknesses?

• **Get External Feedback:** Your friends and family members will have insights into your personality that you yourself don't because in general, we don't see ourselves in the same way as those around us do. By asking people for feedback about how they view you, you will gain a deeper awareness of how you come across to others. While external feedback is important, it is essential that you examine it with a critical eye to ensure you don't become consumed with the opinions of others. Don't just take the information you receive at face value—ask questions. A good question to ask when it comes to the negatives is, "How would you have liked me to behave?" Because if your behavior is continuously causing offense, you will need to reevaluate it.

- **Ask Yourself What:** When dealing with internal conflict, we focus on the "why?" But in most cases, it is difficult to answer because it involves psychoanalyzing yourself, and the average person doesn't have the tools to do that. To cope with these internal conflicts, we play guessing games, which don't provide accurate information. The problem with asking ourselves "why" is that it leads to negative thinking because we tend to focus on our insecurities and weaknesses. Many years ago, when I started my first job, I hated meetings because I was scared of saying anything. When I asked myself why, it was because I was in an entry-level position and I didn't think my co-workers would listen to anything I had to say. The reasons I gave myself were negative. But asking "what" makes you look at your situation objectively so you consider all the factors that could influence the outcome. For instance, instead of asking, "Why am I scared to speak in meetings?" I could ask, "What triggered me to think I wasn't good enough to be taken seriously?" or, "What steps can I take to overcome this fear?"

By asking questions of this nature, you can evaluate your beliefs and behaviors directly and examine them for what they are. Self-awareness enables us to analyze our behavioral patterns and the old stories we tell ourselves, so we can move on from them.

Invest In Your Skills: If you want more out of life, doing the bare minimum isn't going to cut it. Many years ago, before I decided to change my life, I was one of those people who resented the employees who were promoted before me. I didn't understand why I wasn't getting the same opportunities as the person who hadn't been with the company as long as me. I accused them of rigging the system to climb the corporate ladder. But the reality was that they worked harder than me, both on the job and outside the job. They held certifications I had never even heard of. What were they doing? Investing in their skills.

Investing in your skills helps you develop inner strength because it gives you confidence. When you know you are doing everything in your power to achieve your dreams and become the best version of yourself, it boosts your confidence. The Roman philosopher Seneca said, "Luck is what happens when preparation meets opportunity." Successful people are not lucky; they are prepared. In Chapter 1, I mentioned Steven Spielberg and Jim Carrey. Despite their natural talent, they both invested in their skills, and as a result, they walked into opportunities that led to massive success. They persevered because they trusted that the investment they made in perfecting their craft would eventually pay off. Whatever you are good at, whether it's your career, or a talent you have outside your job, invest in your skills so you remain confident in your abilities and hopeful that you will get the opportunities you need to succeed.

Make New Friends: I will discuss this in more depth in Chapter 7, but for now, I'll say that sometimes your friends can prevent you from becoming more self-aware. At the moment, your friends have accepted you for who you are, and if they are not interested in personal development, they won't want *you* to be either, because personal development means change. Your friends won't want you to change because they will no longer be able to relate to you. Therefore, there is a high chance they will attempt to sabotage your journey by shaming you for wanting to change. If you encounter this problem, don't wait for it to get worse—walk away from such people, because who needs friends who don't want the best for them?

Change Your Perspective: The human spirit is powerful, and you will be amazed at what you can handle when you are determined to be an overcomer. There are many people who have experienced insurmountable tragedy, but their suffering has served them well. As a result of their struggles, they become stronger, more resilient, and determined to make an impact on the world. However, such people are rare; the average person does not believe there is any benefit in suffering and they avoid it at all costs. The problem is that there is not one person on the planet who can escape adversity. At some point, it is going to knock at your door. The question is what do you do when it does? Do you allow it to destroy you, or do you allow it to take you to greater heights? It's up to you to decide how adversity affects you.

It is important to mention that changing your perspective about adversity does not mean you are in denial about your pain. Suffering doesn't feel good and it's okay to acknowledge your emotions and work through them. Changing your perspective means you have chosen to trust that whatever challenges you face in life will only serve as a stepping stone to make you stronger, wiser, and more resilient.

Speak to Yourself: You might look a little crazy speaking to yourself, but trust me, it is medicine to the soul. We all have an inner voice that's like a broken record because it is constantly speaking. The problem is that we are not aware of this until we pay attention to it. Unfortunately, for many of us, this voice is not a friendly, comforting voice telling us how awesome we are. It is a hateful and mean voice telling us that we will never amount to anything in life, and that we are wasting time trying to change because the condition we are currently in is what we deserve. This is the voice we hear the majority of the time because most of us are battling with unresolved trauma. Our inner voice is on autopilot and it doesn't stop until we make it stop. Unless we absolutely hated someone, we would never speak to anyone the way we speak to ourselves. People are literally stuck in an emotionally abusive relationship with themselves and it's going to take a lot of work to get out of it.

One way to get started with shutting down your negative inner voice is to recite positive affirmations about yourself. They will help you overcome self-doubt, self-sabotage, and fear. With consistency, you will start believing that you are capable of achieving anything you put your mind to. Here are some affirmations you can start repeating today:

- I have the inner strength to overcome any challenges that I will face in life.

- Every difficulty I experience makes me more resilient and strong.

- I believe I am more than capable of handling life's challenges with courage and grace.

- As I practice developing my inner strength, it continues growing and empowers me to succeed.

- I am confident I will achieve my goals, no matter how challenging they might be.

- I possess unshakeable resilience, and I will always thrive in the midst of life's challenges.

- I am courageous enough to face my fears and turn every negative situation into a positive one.

- I am in control of my emotions and I don't allow them to dictate my actions.

- Each day, I become a stronger and more confident version of myself.

To get into the habit of developing a more positive mindset, say these affirmations out loud every day. Let me warn you that when you start saying these affirmations, everything in you will scream at you to stop because you will feel as if you are lying to yourself—which essentially you are, because at the moment, you hold a completely different belief system. However, if you continue repeating affirmations to yourself every day, what you believe about yourself will change over time. Get into a habit of repeating affirmations daily as well as each time you catch your inner voice speaking negatively.

Expect More: I like gambling. No, I'm not an addict; it's just something I do every once in a while. I don't advise anyone to gamble if you don't have the self-control to quit while you are ahead. When I slap my money down on the table, I do so with expectancy—I expect to win! I don't gamble passively by just playing along and hoping for the best; I expect to get a return on my investment. My expectancy is driven by knowledge; I have studied the game, I understand it, and so my moves are strategic. Life is a game, and you can play to win or be a passive bystander just hoping for the best. The choice is yours. Think about what you truly want out of life, and dare to be audacious about it. I did. I decided that I was going to become a number one bestselling author—and that is exactly what happened. I expected more, and I got more.

Don't Look Back: With the advancement of technology, there is one thing I know for sure: We will never be able to hit the rewind button and go back in time in order to erase our mistakes and start over. Since it is never going to happen, what is the point in lamenting over the past? Whatever mistakes you have made, you can't fix them. But I'll tell you what you *can* do: you can learn from them. Let me ask you a question. What would happen if you drove your car while constantly looking in the rear-view mirror? I am assuming you answered that you would crash, right? That's correct; you would destroy everything in front of you because you were too concerned with what was going on behind you. The rear-view mirror isn't designed for you to keep looking in it; it's there so you can occasionally check what's going on behind you, but your main focus should be what's going on in front of you. Every so often, look back and remind yourself where you've come from, but don't stay there. Keep looking forward to the glorious future that awaits you.

Stop Getting Offended: I have always been very argumentative, and if I heard that anyone was talking smack about me, I would confront them. I know highly sensitive people and empaths are typically not confrontational, but they do take things to heart. I was always offended about something someone said, and I would carry that weight on my shoulders, despite the fact that the person who said what they said had long forgotten that they had said it. It took me a while, but I soon had the revelation that offense is a waste of time and energy, because no matter how awesome you are, there are always going to be people who don't like you. The nicest, funniest, most talented people have haters, and that's okay. First of all, the world is a melting pot, and everyone has different tastes and standards; therefore, it is literally impossible to be everyone's cup of tea. Off topic, but being a people pleaser is the reason a lot of individuals get trapped in abusive relationships with narcissists. Narcissists are constantly moving the goalposts. One day they will complain that they don't like your hair, and so you change it; the next, they don't like the smell of your shampoo, so you change it; next, they don't like the way you dress, and so you change it. Basically, a narcissist will never accept you for who you are and so there is no point in changing yourself to try to please them. The same goes for life in general—be yourself and stop trying to please everyone.

When I wrote my first book, it got mixed reviews; some people loved it, others hated it. But there were more lovers than haters. Initially, I tried to please the haters by editing my book according to their standards, but there were some people who still didn't like it. I eventually came to the conclusion that no matter how I tweaked my writing style, there were always going to be people who didn't like it. Instead of trying to please people, I focused on improving my writing skills and remained authentic.

Similarly, by starting this journey, you are going to rub a lot of people up the wrong way. The closest people to you won't understand why you've chosen this life path, and they will attempt to pull you back into the box they want you to remain in. I will talk more about this in Chapter 7, but they will say some pretty mean things to you and it will take everything in your power not to strike back in anger. Listen; this journey is super hard, and you are going to need every ounce of strength to stay on track—therefore, you can't afford to waste your energy on offense. Let it go!

Embrace Change: Like adversity, change is something we can't control because sometimes, life just does what it wants. The Greek philosopher Heraclitus once said, "The only constant in life is change." As such, it is essential that you embrace it—otherwise, when it comes, you will feel as if the rug has been pulled from underneath your feet. It took me a long time to embrace change because I enjoyed being comfortable. I liked my routine and the predictability of my life. For many people, change, when it is unexpected, is seen as negative, and it can cause fear and anxiety. However, even if change is not something you want, it can be a positive thing if you allow it to be. At my last job, I had the same manager for over ten years. I knew what she expected of me, I knew what to expect from her, and everything in the office ran smoothly. Unfortunately, my manager died in a car accident—one minute she was there, the next she was gone. I was devastated. Not only did I grieve the loss of my manager; I grieved the loss of work as I knew it. At first, I didn't like my new manager. As far as I was concerned, he was too harsh. But I soon discovered that his harshness was his way of pushing his employees to reach their full potential. As much as I loved my former manager, she allowed us to coast, and I got away with doing the bare minimum. With my new manager, my productivity soared because he didn't tolerate slackness. I became more disciplined, and learned way more about the company because of him. In life, flexibility is essential; you must learn how to adapt to any situation because you never know what's going to happen next. Here are some tips on how to embrace change:

- **Confront Fear:** While it's true that fear doesn't feel good, it's important to confront it and do what is necessary to mitigate your fears. Change triggers fear because we don't know what to expect, but if you can prepare yourself for it, your fear won't consume you. For example, let's say your job has just introduced performance-based pay and you're afraid you won't get paid as much as you used to. Work on improving your skills so that your performance is up to scratch. The more confident you are in your abilities, the less fear you will have about your performance.

- **Be Optimistic:** Being optimistic about something you don't want is easier said than done. But it is possible. You might not like change, but there are many great things that can come from it. The next time you experience a shift in your life, instead of focusing on the negative, write down all the benefits that can come from it. For example, you may need to move back into your parents' house because you just got fired from your job. One of the benefits of this is that you will no longer need to stress about paying bills. It will give you the opportunity to save so you can get back on your feet.

- **Relinquish Control:** Trying to have complete control over your situation makes change difficult because in life, there are some things that you can't control. When you are facing uncertainty, you feel safer when you have a sense of control over your situation. Logically, this makes sense, but in order to experience true peace, detaching yourself from the outcome is the most powerful thing you can do. Letting go means you understand that the only thing you have control over is how you think, your attitude, and how you react to the things that are taking place in your life. Once you let go, you can focus your time and energy on the things you *can* control.

When I decided to surrender to the unknown, I was terrified, but I knew I had to do it. To kickstart my journey, I went skydiving. Despite the fear I experienced at the mere thought of throwing myself out of an airplane, it was the most liberating day of my life. I knew I was capable of letting go and allowing the winds of life to direct me where I needed to go, and that is exactly what has happened ever since. I have cruised through life without a care in the world because I trust that whatever happens, I will be all right in the end. That is what letting go is all about—trusting that everything happens for a reason, and even if you don't like what you are going through, it's temporary; you won't be in that situation forever.

Inner strength is one of the most important character traits you can have because it shields you against the turbulence of life. If you are going to become the person you were destined to be, you will need to take the path of least resistance, and doing so is very difficult. It takes a lot of strength and determination not to follow the crowd, and essentially, that is what society values—people who conform to the norms and standards of their environment. But I am assuming that, because you are reading this book, you have chosen a different route, and I applaud you for that because it is not an easy journey. What you are going to need is resilience, and in Chapter 2, I am going to teach you how to build it.

CHAPTER 2:

THINK AND GROW RICH: DEVELOPING A RESILIENT MINDSET

borrowed the name of this chapter title from the book *Think and Grow Rich* by Napoleon Hill. He wrote his book after studying the lives of ordinary people who had become extremely successful. He discovered they all had one thing in common: They believed they could make it. Once they decided on a goal, they put all their time, energy, and efforts into achieving it, and it was this mindset that led to them becoming self-made millionaires. Hill didn't just study one or two people; he studied more than five hundred individuals over a twenty-year span. So what does this have to do with developing a resilient mindset? A resilient mindset is rare; not many people possess it. It's priceless, something money can't buy. Real riches are not monetary—they are the character traits you need in order to live a life of overflow and abundance. Everything starts in the mind. The moment you decide you want a better life for yourself than the one you are currently living, you will get it. In this chapter, you are going to learn how to develop a mind of steel so you become unstoppable.

What Is Resilience?

We are not born with resilience; it is a skill we develop as we go through life. Some people develop it unconsciously, while others choose to learn it. Resilience is essential because it helps us manage life's challenges and thrive despite the adversity we face. Whether it's dealing with major life setbacks, or normal everyday stressors, a resilient mindset will help transform your perspective about life's problems. It will give you the strength to bounce back from adversity, embrace change, and keep doing life to the best of your ability. Resilient people are solutions-oriented; they acknowledge their troubles but remain hopeful that something good will come out of it. Resilience is about having the courage to keep working on your goals despite the obstacles. Resilience empowers you to navigate the trials of life with grace and poise.

Hindrances to Resilience

Developing a resilient mindset is going to be difficult because it's not something you are used to. Most people are used to struggling through adversity, allowing it to hold them back for the rest of their lives. I know many people who were never the same after tragedy struck. Now, I am in no way trying to minimize anyone's pain because I totally understand how difficult life can be. My mother died of a heart attack when I was in my teens, my sister is disabled, and my first husband got another woman pregnant during the first year of our marriage—so, trust and do believe, I've been through some difficult times. It wasn't until I hit rock bottom that I decided enough was enough and I was going to use everything I had been through as fuel to achieve my goals and inspire others. Here are some of the main hindrances to resilience:

A Fixed Mindset: Psychologist Carol Dweck first coined the terms *fixed and growth mindsets* during her study of human motivation. Dweck discovered that people with a growth mindset believe that intelligence and abilities can be developed. Therefore, they make the effort to learn new skills and improve. People with a fixed mindset believe there is nothing you can do about your intelligence or abilities because they are fixed. You either have it or you don't. As a result, they don't bother trying.

People: I've said this before, and I will say it again: When you decide to change your life, the people closest to you won't like it. They are comfortable with their position in life, and they want you to remain comfortable with yours. Change means you are going to leave them behind and they don't want that. Whether consciously or unconsciously, they will try and sabotage your progress. It is very easy for people to knock you off course because building resilience is hard; you are stepping out of your comfort zone, and it is a lot easier to stay there. When your nearest and dearest start challenging your new way of thinking and your hopeful language, what they say will make sense because it lines up with your old way of thinking.

Learning a new skill is similar to the way a plant grows. You plant the seeds, and water and fertilize the seeds for several weeks before you see any sign of growth. By looking at the soil, you can't see anything happening. But beneath the surface, the plant is growing roots so it will be strong enough to sustain itself when it grows. If you stop watering the seeds before the roots form, the plant will never grow. Likewise, when you start learning how to build resilience, you won't see the results immediately, but the more you apply what you learn, the stronger you will become.

The people in your life will either help you water the seeds of resilience you have planted, or they will kill them. When you realize they are killing your seeds, it's up to you to take the required action to either shut them out of your life completely, or keep them at arm's length.

Self-Discipline: Self-discipline is one of the most important life skills you can possess. Without it, everything else fails. You need self-discipline to manage your finances, look after your health, develop healthy relationships, manage your emotions, climb the career ladder and much more. Without self-discipline, you will quickly slip back into your old habits. Again, self-discipline is not a skill you were born with—it is something you learn. Here are a few quick tips to get you started:

- Start with small acts of self-control like drinking a glass of water with your lunch instead of Coke.

- Don't look at your phone for the first hour after waking up in the morning.

- Make your bed every morning.

- Create a short daily routine and stick to it for seven days. Once you hit seven days, extend it for another seven days. Keep doing this until your daily routine becomes a habit.

I will leave it at that so as not to overwhelm you. These things might seem small, but they are powerful. These small actions will lead to greater ones. The more you practice, the stronger your self-discipline will become.

HOW TO DEVELOP RESILIENCE

According to the Calm website, the foundation for building resilience is to possess the Seven C's of resilience:

1. **Competence:** This means that, because you know difficult times are going to come, you prepare for them in advance by developing the skills required to face challenges.

2. **Confidence:** Everyone can be confident when life is going well, but do you have that same confidence when everything is going wrong?

3. **Connection:** The worst kind of people to have in your life are those with a weak mindset because they can't help you when the storms of life are raging. They might mean well, but they have nothing to offer other than helping you to dig the pit of self-pity even deeper.

4. **Character:** Your true character is revealed during times of adversity. Everyone can be of good character when things are going well for them. You won't know who you really are until you are in the fire.

5. **Contribution:** Doing things to improve the lives of others, whether through volunteering, helping out a neighbor, or donating money to an organization; having a sense of purpose is empowering because you are stepping outside of yourself.

6. **Coping:** Learning how to cope with stress is essential during difficult times. Healthy coping strategies ensure that your struggles don't overwhelm you.

7. **Control:** As mentioned in Chapter 1, focusing on the things you can't control leaves you feeling powerless. But when you choose to relinquish control and allow the universe to do its thing, you stop feeling so helpless and gain the strength required to take action on the things you *can* control.

Find Your Purpose: I believe that every single human being on Earth was born with a purpose. First, let's discuss what purpose means. According to the *Oxford Dictionary*, purpose means, "The reason for which something is done or created or for which something exists." For example, a car was created to carry people to and from their chosen destination. A cup was created to drink from. A plate was created to eat off. Do you get my point? What were human beings created to do? According to society, we were created to be slaves to a capitalist system. To work, pay bills, retire when we have a few more years to live, and die! Does that sound like a fulfilling life to you? Sometimes, when I walk through the streets, I take a good look at people's faces, and do you know what I see the majority of the time? Misery. People are miserable because they are not doing what they were created to do.

Time and time again, studies have found that those who are doing what they were created to do are the happiest and most fulfilled in life. Why? Because you feel complete; there is no void you are trying to fill. You get up every morning with a plan, and you are making an impact in people's lives. Purpose brings joy, a deep feeling of meaning and passion that you won't find anywhere else. Money can't provide it. Fame can't provide it. Nothing in this world can give you what purpose can—because your purpose is what you were created to do. Most people haven't found their life's purpose because it's not something they've ever thought about. Some people have a deep knowing that they were created to do more, and others have just accepted that there is nothing more to life than the one they are currently living. If you want to know how to find your purpose, keep reading.

- **Self-Reflection:** Life is so fast-paced that most people have never taken the time to get to know themselves. Getting to know yourself is the first step to finding your purpose. Spend time reflecting on your strengths, weaknesses, interests, and values. What are the things that bring you a sense of meaning, fulfilment and joy? By asking yourself these critical questions, you will begin to form an idea of the direction you need to take.

- **Your Talents:** Everyone is born with at least one talent and it is not limited to singing, dancing, or acting. You might be a good problem-solver, artist, cook, listener, writer, communicator, hair stylist, or makeup artist. Your talent is connected to your purpose. Find it, and you've found your purpose.

- **Your Passions:** Some people are multitalented, which can get confusing when finding your purpose. It was my mentor who told me my purpose was connected to my talent, and the first thing I said to her was that I've got more than one talent. I can write, I can draw, and I'm an athlete. Her response was, "Which one of those are you most passionate about?" My passion has always been writing—it was back then and it still is now. The same applies to you; if you have more than one talent, your purpose is connected to the talent you are most passionate about.

- **Decision Time:** Now that you know what your purpose is, it's time to decide how you are going to live it out. Are you going to become a hairdresser, an artist, or a chef? If so, how far do you want to go with it? Your next step is planning and goal-setting; I will go into detail about goal-setting in Chapter 5.

- **Practice:** In Chapter 1, I wrote about Jim Carrey and Steven Spielberg. Both of them knew what their purpose was from an early age, and they invested a lot of time and energy into perfecting their craft. That's what you need to do. Some people assume that, because they are naturally good at something, they don't need to practice. In fact, talent can make you quite arrogant. The girl who can hit notes as high as Mariah Carey might assume she doesn't need singing lessons. But what she doesn't understand is that, although singing is a natural gift, it is also a skill, and the more you practice, the better you will become at it. All singers have a voice coach—even the late Whitney Houston had one, and she was probably one of the greatest singers of all time. Whatever you are good at, start practicing, and remember, "Luck is when preparation meets opportunity." ~Seneca

Believe in Yourself: Sometimes, I despise the world we live in because it is responsible for making people so insecure that they never flourish. Society has programmed us to conform to a certain standard, and if you don't fit it, you are considered an outcast. Young children are bullied relentlessly in school because they don't fit the mold. Suicide amongst children is on the increase, according to the Centers for Disease Control and Prevention. In America, in 2020, over 500 children between the ages of ten and fourteen years old died by suicide. There are several reasons children are taking their own lives, and counsellors suggest one reason is social media use.

Large numbers of children own a cell phone by elementary school, and they spend all their free time staring at a screen. They stay up all hours of the night scrolling. One of the consequences of this is online bullying. Plus they are constantly exposed to glamorous lifestyles, which leads to comparison, which then leads to insecurity, which then leads to depression. Children are way too young to manage such heavy emotions, hence the suicide rates. I said all that to say this: Negative programing starts at a young age. Most of you reading this have probably carried your childhood insecurity into your adult years. You don't have to play the hand you were dealt—you can put your cards down and pick up new ones, the cards that you want to play with. You are in the driver's seat of your destiny; how your life turns out is completely up to you. Building resilience requires you to believe in yourself, because if you don't, you will constantly look to others for validation, which is terrible for your mental health. Here are some tips on how to believe in yourself:

Improve Your Health: An unhealthy body equals an unhealthy mind. Before I get my head taken off by the body-positivity-movement crew, this isn't about body shaming. I am well aware that some people are overweight because they have health issues they have no control over. I'm not talking about them. I'm talking about the people who know they have unhealthy eating habits and want to change. I'm referring to these people because I used to be one of them. I knew full well that my diet was killing me, but I had a food addiction and I had to put the work in to overcome it. I was in a constant battle with food and achieving my goals. Eating unhealthy food made me extremely lazy. I'm not going to go into the science of it here, but many studies have found that processed foods, sugar, and white carbohydrates sap your energy levels, making you less motivated to do anything. I can testify that this is true. After eating a whole pizza and downing a couple of cans of soda, the only energy I had was to move my fingers for the purpose of changing the channel or scrolling! If I managed to get through a thirty-day challenge of no fast food, I had boundless energy, my mind was sharp, and I would consistently get stuff done. But one relapse, and it was over for me. I kept taking two steps forward and then ten steps back.

I eventually kicked my food addiction and got into the best shape of my life. One of the things that motivated me to stay on track was how I started plowing through my goals. Unhealthy food literally rots the brain—with every chip, sip of soda, and bite of a burger, I was killing myself. I am amazed at the difference in my mindset now I've permanently changed my diet. It's like I'm a completely different person.

Nurture Yourself: Most people don't take care of themselves because they don't have time. We are so busy ripping and running that self-care is an alien concept. There is more to self-care than going to a spa, getting a massage, or going on vacation once a year. It is something you should practice consistently because it helps avoid burnout and reestablish balance in your life. When you're tired, frustrated, and overwhelmed, you are more likely to give up when the storms of life hit. Self-care involves taking care of yourself physically, mentally, socially, and spiritually.

- **Mental:** Many people are struggling with mental health today, and you might be one of them. If so, I advise that you seek professional help immediately. Even after you stop seeing a therapist, be sure to make taking care of your mental health a priority. It has only been recently that mental health has become a commonplace topic in the media. A few years back, you never heard about it. Society indirectly teaches us that our physical appearance is the most important thing in life. We are bombarded with images of attractive people that have been so airbrushed that it's impossible to ever look like that. The problem is worse for women because we have been conditioned to believe that unless we fit a certain standard of beauty, we are worthless. Unfortunately, many women believe this, which just adds to the mental health crisis.

- **Emotional:** Emotions such as sadness, anxiety, and anger are valid emotions, and you are allowed to feel and experience them. Unfortunately, most of us are taught to suppress these emotions in favor of a fake smile. I know I was. As a child, I was constantly shut down if I expressed negative emotions. So, guess what—as an adult, I did the same. The inability to regulate your emotions is extremely unhealthy. Not only is it bad for our mental health; it destroys relationships. Educate yourself about your emotions and how to manage them. Here are some books that really helped me on my emotional-healing journey.

  - *The Emotion Code: How to Release Your Trapped Emotions for Abundant Health, Love and Happiness* by Dr. Bradley Nelson
  - *Destructive Emotions: How Can We Overcome Them? A Scientific Dialogue With the Dalai Lama* by Daniel Goleman
  - *Don't Blame the Brain: The Missing Link Between Emotions and Inner Peace* by Julia Pappas
  - *Master Your Emotions: A Practical Guide to Overcome Negativity and Better Manage Your Feelings* by Thibaut Meurisse
  - *Unglued: Making Wise Choices in the Midst of Raw Emotions* by Lysa TerKeurst

Remember, application is the key to success. There is no point in reading these books if you are not going to apply what you learn.

- **Physical:** Before I started my self-help journey, I was always sick with the flu, migraines, and stomach bugs. I was always on one medication or another, which caused side effects such as gum disease, thinning hair, acne, and a host of other problems. My problem wasn't sickness—it was that I wasn't taking care of my health, and that was causing the sickness. When I changed my diet and started exercising consistently, all my ailments disappeared. Physical self-care involves healthy eating, exercise, getting enough sleep, getting health checkups, and going to the dentist. Take control of your health now, before you lose complete control of it. Remember, a healthy body equals a healthy mind.

- **Social:** Relationships are important, and a busy life often leads to us neglecting them. When we don't make time for friends and family, our connections begin to dwindle. Close connections are essential for our overall well-being. To cultivate your relationships, you must invest in them. We all have different social needs. Work out what yours are and make time to socialize. How often you socialize is up to you; it could be once a week, once every two weeks, or once a month. Decide what works best for you and your social group and go from there.

- **Spiritual:** People tend to become more spiritual when something bad happens. For example, many pastors stated that their churches were jam-packed after the terrorist attacks on September 11th. However, it was short-lived—once the grief had subsided, the seats were empty again. Nurturing your spirit is not something you do when tragedy strikes; it should be a part of your daily routine. One of the reasons people turn to spirituality when something bad happens is because it strengthens you and gives you the courage to keep moving forward. If that is the case, wouldn't it make sense to adopt spiritual practices daily? When people hear the word "spiritual," they assume it means religion. While it can refer to religion, you don't need to be religious to be spiritual. Spirituality is about developing a deeper sense of meaning in life by connecting with something that is greater than you. Some people choose to connect with the universe, tap into energy, or practice the law of attraction. Whatever way you choose to become more spiritual, make it a daily habit.

Improve Your Problem-Solving Skills: It is the way you think about challenges and problems that helps you build resilience. A person with good problem-solving skills will look for solutions when the obstacles arise. The best problem solvers think outside the box. They use their creative, analytical, and practical skills to find solutions. Psychologist Abraham Maslow once said, "If the only tool you have is a hammer, you tend to see every problem as a nail." This quote came from a concept called "the law of the instrument," which is when people rely on one way of doing things—and that is typically what is most comfortable for them. Learning new ways of thinking and doing things is essential for overcoming challenges. Resilience is built when you have confidence in your problem-solving skills because you trust you will eventually find your way out of the situation. Here's how to improve your problem-solving skills:

- **Understand:** Albert Einstein, who was probably the greatest problem solver of all time, once said, "If I had an hour to solve a problem, I'd spend fifty-five minutes thinking about the problem and five minutes thinking about the solutions." Problems go unsolved because there has not been enough time spent understanding them. If you don't understand the problem you are facing, you'll have a very difficult time finding a solution. As Einstein said, it might take a while to understand the problem, but the solution will come to you a lot faster once you do. Some people struggle with problem solving because they are so eager to find a solution to get out of their situation that they invest more time looking for a solution than they do understanding the problem.

- **Brainstorm:** Brainstorming isn't about finding the right solution; it's about using your critical-thinking skills to evaluate solutions from different perspectives. Stop focusing on how you have always done things—focus on changing your thinking and finding new solutions.

- **Identify:** After brainstorming, decide on the best solution by evaluating the pros and cons. Consider how it is going to solve the problem, and what the end result will look like.

- **Action Plan:** Don't rush into implementation, because you might have the right solution but the wrong process for implementing it. Therefore, get an action plan in place where you develop a step-by-step process for implementation.

- **Measure:** Once you have implemented the solution, measure its progress. If it works, great. If not, start working on another solution.

Develop Your Locus of Control: According to psychologist Julian Rotter, the pioneer of the term "locus of control," people either believe they are in control over the events that happen in their lives or they are not in control of them. People have either one of the following:

- **Internal Locus of Control:** The belief that you are in the driver's seat of your life and that whatever happens to you is because of your choices and efforts. For example, you got the job you wanted because you spent weeks studying for the interview. Had you not prepared for the interview, and didn't get the job, you have owned the fact that you didn't get hired because your interview performance was mediocre due to your lack of preparation.

- **External Locus of Control:** The belief that outside forces control your life, and that you have no control over what happens to you. For example, you believe you didn't get the job you wanted because you were discriminated against for your sexuality.

There are many advantages to having an internal locus of control, such as:

- **You Take Accountability:** No one goes through life without making mistakes. Those who believe they are in control of their life own their mistakes and learn from them. You will never learn if you are always blaming your mistakes on external forces.

- **You Are Self-Motivated:** You don't sit around waiting for handouts—you take action. When you set a goal for yourself, you keep working on it until you achieve it.

- **You Possess Self-Efficacy:** People with a high level of self-efficacy believe they are capable of succeeding. As a result, they do what they need to do to get stuff done. They believe they are responsible for creating the miracles they want to see in their lives.

- **You Are Open to Constructive Criticism:** The purpose of constructive criticism is to help you become a better person. Those who want to improve their lives will welcome constructive criticism with open arms. They will take the advice and run with it.

- **Better Mental Health:** Playing the blame game damages your mental health because you are always thinking the worst. When you don't believe you have control over your life, you are constantly looking over your shoulder and expecting something bad to happen. However, believing you are in control over your life alleviates you from the stress and worry of the belief that you may never achieve anything because some external forces are pulling the strings. Additionally, people with an internal locus of control are more likely to focus on healthy habits that are good for their mental health.

On the other hand, people with an external locus of control are more likely to do the following:

- Give up on their dreams when things are not going their way because they believe that the obstacles mean it wasn't meant to be.

- Give up on their relationships because they believe there is nothing they can do to make things right.

- Remain in bad situations because they don't believe there is anything they can do to change things.

- Point the finger at other people or the powers that be when things go wrong.

- When things go well, they put it down to a fluke even if they put the work in.

If you have an external locus of control and believe that external forces are working against you, it's time for a shift in mentality. Here are some things you can do to develop an internal locus of control:

- **Take Accountability:** The next time you make a mistake, take accountability for your actions. Before pointing the finger, stop and think about the things you may have done that contributed to what went wrong. For example, you are ten minutes late for work and your boss pulls you up about it. Your excuse is that you got stuck in traffic, which is true. But the reality is that you hit the snooze button for an hour before getting out of bed. You don't need to tell your manager this, but what you can do is apologize and promise that it won't happen again.

- **Focus on Solutions:** When something doesn't go your way, instead of fixating on the problem, focus on the solution. Focusing on the problem is a waste of time and energy because thinking about it isn't going to change it. If you want to lose weight, do you sit down thinking about the weight you want to lose? Sounds ridiculous, doesn't it? But that's what happens when you focus on the problem. The problem isn't going to disappear by itself, it's up to you to fix it.

- **Set Goals:** Build your confidence in your internal locus of control by setting small goals and achieving them. A small goal might be to challenge yourself for thirty days to wash the dishes every night before going to bed. Setting small goals and achieving them will help you realize that the only person who was stopping you previously was you. There are no external forces holding you back. Now you can see that, when you are willing to do the work, you can achieve anything you set your mind to.

- **Learn New Skills:** Learning new skills forces you to step outside your comfort zone. People with an external locus of control prefer to remain in their comfort zone because that's where they feel safe. By forcing yourself to learn something new, you are training your mind to believe in yourself and your capabilities because *you* are the one doing the work required to become better at the skill you are learning. A new skill could be to learn how to play a musical instrument, or to learn a new language.

- **Reframe Failures:** People who play the blame game don't learn from failure because as far as they're concerned, the failure wasn't their fault. They don't look into it deep enough to get anything positive out of it. Failure is an essential part of success because without it, there is no growth. It makes you work harder and seek new ways of doing things. It took Thomas Edison many attempts to make a light bulb. During an interview, when asked how he felt about all the failures he had had, he said, "I have not failed; I've just found ten thousand ways that won't work." Once you reframe failure, it won't scare you anymore.

Resilience will help you get to the next level of your self-development journey because it strengthens you to continue despite the setbacks. The reality is that becoming the best version of yourself is hard, and you will have many struggles along the way. The more resilient you are, the more determined you will be to crush the goals you set for yourself.

Another component of self-development is confidence, because if you don't believe in yourself, you won't believe you are capable of achieving anything worthwhile. Successful people are extremely confident. If you want to live the life of your dreams, confidence is a must. In Chapter 3, I will teach you how to develop unshakable confidence.

CHAPTER 3:

STAND TALL: HOW TO DEVELOP UNSHAKABLE CONFIDENCE

Approximately eighty percent of women struggle with confidence, reports a study by the National Bureau of Economic Research. According to the Women's Confidence Report, very few women feel extremely confident, with just three to four percent of global participants rating their confidence at a nine to ten. The same report found that seventy-eight percent of American women gain their confidence from external validation, which has mental health consequences such as stress, depression, and relationship conflicts. The evidence suggests that women in general struggle with confidence. Why is this? Let's find out.

In a world that constantly challenges our sense of self, developing confidence can be extremely difficult. I've spent a lot of time studying confidence, and found that most experts don't believe it's an innate trait. However, while I don't have any research to back up what I'm saying, my critical thinking has led me to a different conclusion. Let me explain. A baby cries because they can't speak and that's how they get the attention of their caregivers. Whether consciously or unconsciously, they have full confidence that they are going to get what they need when they turn the waterworks on. Toddlers are fearless; they put anything in their mouths, touch everything, and will topple headfirst down a flight of stairs if they want something. Once they start talking, they will confidently tell you what they want and need. Toddlers speak to anyone; they will wave at you from the car window, or walk up to a total stranger and ask for a bite of their sandwich. Toddlers have no concept of insecurity. But at around five years old, things change and children start becoming less confident.

Babies are born with confidence and then they lose it. What happens? There are many reasons why children become insecure, and it starts in the home. Some parents are physically, mentally, and emotionally abusive. Others might not be abusive but they subject their children to such high standards that it makes them insecure when they don't achieve them. Then there's school; some children get bullied for all sorts of reasons, including looking different, not wearing the right clothes, or not being good at sports. All these things contribute to sapping the confidence out of children.

Highly sensitive and empath children are even more prone to insecurity because their parents are not aware of their personality type and therefore struggle to raise them—and in some cases treat their children as outcasts. This treatment continues in school because they are not the same as the other kids. If highly sensitive and empath children were nurtured the right way, they would flourish. But typically, this isn't the case. They often don't connect with their true identity until adulthood.

While it's true that confidence is something you can learn, it's also true that you were born with it. Essentially, what you are doing is relearning what you already know. It's already in you—you've just got to reach deep inside and pull it back out.

Wow! That was a long introduction. And before we begin, I just want to remind you that you are an awesome human being, and you can achieve anything you put your mind to. With that said, in this chapter, you are going to learn how to develop unshakable confidence.

WORK ON YOUR MENTAL HEALTH

Research suggests there is a strong link between confidence and mental health. Mental illness symptoms make you feel depressed, overwhelmed, and extremely vulnerable. Severe depression causes you to feel that life is pointless and isn't worth living. People suffering from severe anxiety feel so uneasy they find it difficult to function. Mental health disorders get worse if they are left untreated; therefore, it is advised that you get the help you need as soon as possible. Treating a mental health condition will involve one of the following:

- Psychotherapy
- Medication
- Talking therapy
- Self-help

When your mental health starts improving, it will become easier to build your confidence. It is also important to mention that mental health is not just about a condition you have been diagnosed with—it also includes your overall well-being. Here are some tips on how to improve your mental well-being.

- **Connect:** There are several benefits to connecting with your loved ones and friends. Research suggests it makes you less susceptible to depression and anxiety, boosts your self-esteem, and makes you more empathetic. Friends and loved ones celebrate with you during the good times and support you when life isn't so kind. The problem with connections is that sometimes, we can neglect them. We can get so busy that we don't make time for the people we love. While this is not intentional, it can fracture relationships because you grow apart. Whether it's once a week, twice a month, or once a month, make an effort to spend time with friends and loved ones.

- **Exercise:** Physical activity is good for the mind because being active releases hormones called endorphins which are also referred to as, "feel-good hormones." Feeling good is an essential part of improving your well-being.

- **Stay Present:** Staying present involves keeping your mind focused on the moment. Most people are either thinking about the past or the future, and most of the time these thoughts are not healthy. They typically consist of regretting something that happened in the past, or worrying about the future. Living in the present moment involves enjoying what you are doing at that time by focusing solely on the activity you are engaging in. This can be anything from watching television to having a conversation with a friend.

- **Learn:** Learning new things keeps the brain active, and an active brain is a healthy one. We rarely talk about the importance of keeping the brain engaged. There are several ways you can achieve this, including learning a new skill, reading, and playing games such as Sudoku.

- **Volunteer:** Volunteering is a great way to improve your mental well-being because it serves as a reminder that there are people in the world who are suffering a lot more than you. While pain is a relative term, and I am not trying to diminish what you are going through, stepping outside of yourself to help others gives you a sense of meaning and purpose, which gives you hope. Hope gives you the courage to keep going despite the challenges you are facing.

Change Your Body Language

You notice a confident person as soon as they walk into a room because of their body language. According to professor of psychology Albert Mehrabian, fifty-five percent of our communication is nonverbal. You say more with your body language than you do with your words. Even if you are not a body-language expert, you can read people simply by observing how they move. For example, a confident person typically walks with their head up and shoulders back, and they take slow strides with their hands loosely by their sides. An insecure person walks with their head down, shoulders slouched, and their hands either deep in their pockets or their arms pressed against their body. The thing about body language is that it's not something we consciously think about. However, once you realize you are displaying negative body language, you can change it. Here's how to use your body language to appear more confident:

Steeple Your Hands: Steepling is when someone pushes their fingertips together and makes a triangle shape with their hands. You will often see people in positions of power steepling their hands during conversation or when giving a speech. This position makes you look more confident about what you are saying. However, when delivering this pose, the position of your hands is important. When sitting at a table, position your hands closer to your face. When standing up, rest your hands just above your waist. Stay away from the handgun steeple where you point with your thumb and index finger and cross the rest of your fingers, because this can make you seem arrogant and aggressive.

Assertive Posture: An assertive posture involves standing straight with your weight balanced evenly on both feet. Keep your head held high, making sure it is in line with your spine. Relax your shoulders but be careful not to hunch them. If you are speaking to someone, leave space between you—standing too close can be interpreted as an invasion of privacy.

When walking, walk with intention, as if you've got somewhere to go. Avoid taking large strides because this can make you seem aggressive or stressed-out. Also, avoid taking small, hurried steps because you look like a mouse scurrying to get somewhere. Take medium strides and keep your pace even.

Display assertiveness when sitting down by positioning yourself in the middle of the chair. Push the bottom of your spine against the back of the chair and sit up straight. Use the armrests if they are available. Position your feet flat on the floor with your knees pointed in front of you. Don't fold your arms or use your hand to support your head. If there is no table, rest your hands on your lap with your palms facing downwards. If there's a table in front of you, place both hands on the table spaced out with your palms facing downwards.

Facial Expressions: Facial expressions are an important part of body language because they display how you feel. Everyone knows when someone is happy, sad, or angry because of their facial expression. But did you know that your facial expressions can also make you look confident or insecure? Insecure facial expressions include biting your lips, low eyebrows, tucked chin, no eye contact. To improve your facial expressions, do the following:

- Stop yourself from biting your lips by drinking a glass of water before having an important conversation.

- Raise your eyebrows by smiling and opening your eyes fully.

- During a conversation, keep your chin up by taking slow, deep, breaths. Deep breathing expands your body, which will stop your chin from pointing downwards.

Eye Contact: While making eye contact with someone when speaking to them is polite because it shows you are interested in the conversation, it can also be uncomfortable if you are not familiar with the person you are speaking to. However, making eye contact also gives the impression that you are confident. According to a study conducted by the Idiap Research Institute, when a person makes eye contact during conversation, it signifies their dominance and social hierarchy. The study discovered that people who were at the top of the social ladder gave and received more eye contact. It's almost like the person making the eye contact is marking their territory. Another study found that people with high self-esteem broke eye contact less than the participants with low self-esteem.

While it is true that eye contact can make you appear more confident, making too much eye contact can come across as creepy. To make eye contact effectively, do the following:

- Make eye contact before starting the conversation.

- When speaking to someone, spend fifty percent of the time maintaining eye contact. When listening to someone, spend seventy percent of the time maintaining eye contact.

- Maintain eye contact for four to five seconds and then break eye contact. Don't look away too quickly or you will seem nervous. Look over to the side and then divert your eyes back to the person.

- Look away by nodding or gesturing, this is a more natural way to break your gaze.

- If you find it too uncomfortable looking someone directly in the eyes, look at their chin, mouth, or nose.

Stop Fidgeting: Do you do things like shake your leg when you're sitting down, tap the table, or play with the coins in your pocket? Even if you don't mean to, these movements can give off the wrong impression. They can make you appear nervous, bored, or frustrated. Even if they do feel like this, confident people know how to manage their behavior. To avoid fidgeting, replace these bad habits with more productive ones such as taking a few deep breaths to calm your nerves, giving yourself a pep talk, or going for a walk to release nervous energy.

Power Poses: According to social psychologist Amy Cuddy, power posing for two minutes per day makes you feel more confident. A power pose is a stance associated with power, confidence, and achievement. In her 2012 TED Talk, Cuddy explains that power is expressed through our bodies, and that both humans and animals do this. People shrink themselves when they feel insecure and don't want to be seen. When we feel confident, we take up space. Cuddy's study discovered that two minutes of power posing caused an eight-percent increase in testosterone, and two minutes of non-power poses caused a ten-percent decrease in testosterone. Additionally, power posing caused a twenty-five-percent decrease in the stress hormone cortisol, while non-power poses caused a fifteen-percent increase in cortisol. To boost your confidence, add power poses to your daily routine. You can also practice them before an important event like a job interview or a speaking gig. Here are a few you can practice:

- **The Warrior:** This is a pose of resilience, strength, and determination. Spread your feet apart with one foot in front of the other. Secure your stance by bending your knee and planting your feet firmly on the ground. Make a lunge position with your body by lowering it. Lift your arms above your head and stretch them out on either side of you.

- **The Open-Arms:** The open-arms pose is one of confidence, approachability, and openness. Sit or stand with your arms wide apart out by your sides. Lift your chest and your head up.

- **The CEO:** This pose demonstrates leadership and authority. Stand or sit with your legs crossed. With your fingers interlocked, place your hands behind your head. Keep your posture open and lean back slightly.

- **The Victory:** The victory pose symbolizes confidence and triumph. Stand straight and position your feet so they are slightly wider than your hips. Position your hands above your head in the shape of a V. Keep your palms facing outwards.

- **The Wonder Woman:** This pose is a sign of assertiveness, boldness, and bravery. Stand straight with your feet level with your shoulders. Slightly lift your chin up and position your hands on your hips.

Reinvent Yourself

If you are tired of looking in the mirror every day and disliking what you see, it's time to reinvent yourself. One of the reasons your confidence is lacking is because you don't like where you are in life. Perhaps you're in a bad relationship, you hate your job, or you've developed habits that are holding you back. Whatever the reason, reinventing yourself will boost your confidence and improve your outlook on life. If you want to know how to reinvent yourself, keep reading.

Define Your Why: Before getting started on this journey, ask yourself why you want to reinvent yourself. When you have a clear understanding of why, you will develop a stronger desire to accomplish the goals you set for yourself. Your why acts as a source of motivation; it will provide you with the fuel you need to keep going when you feel like giving up. The German philosopher Friedrich Nietzsche said, "He who has a why can endure any how." Basically, you become unstoppable when you have a reason for what you are doing. Reinventing yourself isn't easy—there will be many challenges along the way, and somedays, you will want to throw in the towel. Remaining in your current state is a lot easier than putting in the work required to reinvent yourself. Once you get started, and you realize how difficult it is, everything in you will want to quit and return to your comfortable but miserable life. Anytime you start feeling this way, remember your why.

Evaluate Your Life: Evaluating your life will help you determine how you want to reinvent yourself. Here are some questions to consider during the evaluation process:

- What values do I hold and how does my current lifestyle align with them?

- Which parts of my life am I least satisfied with and why?

- What do I want my future to look like? What actions am I currently taking to make this happen?

- What do I need to learn to achieve the goals I have set for myself?

- Who do I admire and what do I admire about them?

- What limiting beliefs or fears are hindering me from making changes?

- How can my daily routine include more of what I love?

- What legacy do I want to leave?

- What can I do today to start working towards my reinvention?

Make a Plan: Okay, so you have an idea of how you want to re-invent yourself—that's great. But what you need is a solid plan to guide your reinvention. A plan is like a compass, leading you along the path you wish to travel. It is what you return to when you lose your sense of direction and feel lost. A plan will remind you of the next step you need to take in this important journey. I go into detail about goal-setting in Chapter 5. Hold this page, flip to Chapter 5, and create your reinvention plan.

Take Action: Planning is essential for success, but without execution, your plans will be in vain. It's easy to sit down with a pen and paper and write out your plans, but most people never achieve what they set out to because they don't take action. Taking action will be the most difficult part of your reinvention journey because you are stepping out of your comfort zone and taking the steps required become your ideal self. This is a scary process and it will take a lot of courage. But if you are serious about becoming the person you know you were destined to be, take action now.

IMPROVE YOUR PHYSICAL APPEARANCE

Unfortunately, we live in a superficial world, and the reality is that the more physically appealing you are, the better you are treated. Studies have found that on average, attractive people earn more money, it is assumed they are better leaders, more intelligent, and more trustworthy—all of which improve a person's chances of getting the jobs they apply for or getting promoted to higher positions. Another aspect of this is that attractive people exude confidence because they know they are attractive. When you fit the standard of beauty, and you are constantly told how good-looking you are, it only makes sense that you are going to be more confident. I am not suggesting that your looks will determine how confident you are, because I know plenty of insecure attractive people. However, one cannot deny that attractive people are more confident because society has placed them on a pedestal.

Now, not everyone can look like a supermodel; however, you can make yourself look as attractive as possible, because as the saying goes, when you look good, you feel good. Think about how you feel when you are all dressed up for a night out. You are a lot more confident because you know you look good. But when you're making a quick trip to the store wearing an old tracksuit, you don't feel so dapper, do you? I love watching makeover shows where professional stylists and makeup artists completely transform a person's looks. The end result is like night and day; they look like a completely different person. It's the clear boost in confidence that gets me every time. The individual goes from looking like they are carrying the weight of the world on their shoulders to vibrant and energetic and ready to take on the world. To help boost your confidence, work on your physical appearance. Here are some tips:

- **Skincare:** Healthy skin makes you look refreshed and healthy. I used to suffer from terrible acne and it made me extremely insecure. I hated looking at people when I spoke to them, and I walked with my head down so people wouldn't look at me. But once I started taking my health seriously and my skin cleared up, my confidence soared. Your skincare routine doesn't need to be the excessive ten-step ones you see on TikTok. Do some research, choose something that works best for you and stick with it. I've found that a good cleanser, toner, and moisturizer is all I need to maintain a glowing, youthful look.

- **Haircare:** Well-maintained hair makes a big difference to your appearance. Again, keeping your hair well-groomed doesn't necessarily mean getting expensive haircuts, extensions, highlights, etc. If you can afford it, that's great. However, for those of you on a budget, maintain a consistent haircare routine by washing, conditioning, and moisturizing it. Get a good trim at least three times a year.

- **Oral Hygiene:** A nice set of teeth will improve your smile and overall appearance. If you need braces or teeth whitening, go ahead and get that done. Other than that, to maintain good oral hygiene, brush your teeth twice a day, floss, and use mouth wash.

- **Regular Exercise:** Keep yourself in shape through regular exercise. If you know you need to lose a few pounds, work on that. Regular exercise doesn't necessarily mean going to the gym. You can jog, skip, or do a home workout. There are plenty of personal trainers on YouTube who provide free workouts. Take a look and see what suits you the best. The World Health Organization (WHO) advises that adults do at least 150-300 minutes of moderate-intensity physical exercise per week.

- **Nutrition:** Good nutrition plays an important role in improving your appearance because it supports your overall health and well-being. For example, when it comes to the condition of your skin, you can use all of the most expensive products, but if you're eating junk food every day and not drinking enough water, your skin won't clear up. Experts suggest ditching the standard American diet of ultra-processed foods, sodium, and added sugar in favor of lean protein, legumes, whole grains, fruits, and vegetables.

- **Dress Well:** The icing on the cake is your clothing. Stylish, well-fitting clothes not only make you look good, but they make you feel good. You don't need to buy expensive clothes to dress well. Personal stylist Lauren Messiah suggests that one of the best things you can do for your look is dress according to your size. You don't need to be wafer-thin to look stylish; it's okay if you've got some meat on your bones—just make sure you wear the right clothes for your shape. To dress well on a budget, avoid the latest trends and invest in classic pieces instead. According to HarpersBazaar.com, here are fifteen classic fashion pieces every woman should own:

1. White shirt

2. Leather handbag

3. Trench coat

4. Long black dress

5. A watch

6. Court shoes

7. Hoop earrings

8. White sneakers

9. Breton top

10. Strappy heels

11. Leather jacket

12. Cashmere knit

13. Trouser suit

14. Camel coat

15. Denim jeans

Avoid the Things That Make You Feel Insecure

For most of us, the seeds of insecurity were planted during our childhood. Unfortunately, whether knowingly or unknowingly, our parents were responsible for destroying our confidence. Sometimes, it is the people closest to us who contribute to our feelings of unworthiness. Additionally, we are forced to deal with conforming to societal expectations of how we are meant to show up in the world. If we don't conform to the standards that have been forced upon us, we are ridiculed. While we can't hide away from the world because we've got to live in it, we can choose to avoid the things that make us feel insecure. Here's how:

Identify Your Triggers: The first step in avoiding the things that make you feel insecure is to identify your triggers. These are some of the things you should pay attention to:

- **Inner Critic:** Your inner critic is that little voice in your soul that pops up to remind you that you are not good enough. Pay attention to your negative thought patterns to determine when your inner critic is harassing you. It will reveal your insecurities to you so you know what to avoid. For example, when you're on your way to meet one of your toxic friends or family members, your inner critic might start saying something like, "You better not wear that tight top and show your fat stomach because Stacy will remind you of how much weight you're putting on." That's one way to determine that you are hanging around toxic people; your inner critic will make you feel anxious about going to meet up with them.

- **Emotional Reactions:** There are certain situations that will make you feel insecure, and the emotional reaction you have will serve as an indication that you are in the wrong environment. You might feel nervous when out at a bar, and only relax once you get a couple of drinks in you. If you need to get tipsy to have a good time, you might need to change how you choose to have fun.

- **Physical Symptoms:** Do you feel sick, sweaty, or shaky when you get around certain people, places, or things? This could be because you are in a situation that makes you feel insecure.

- **Journal:** Keeping a journal will help you tune into your insecurities. Anytime you are in a situation where you start doubting yourself, feel anxious, or nervous, write about it. By writing about your behavioral responses, you will gain deeper insight into the things that make you feel insecure so you can stay away from them.

Avoid Toxic People: Unfortunately for me, my family members are very toxic. They are extremely negative and would rather sit around complaining about how unfair the world is than do the work required to create the life that they desire. When I started writing my first book, I was so excited and naturally wanted to share my excitement with my loved ones. But all I got was, "How are you going to write a book? You don't even have a publisher. You haven't been trained... blah, blah, blah." They had nothing positive to say at all. When I became a bestseller, the negativity didn't stop. I had hoped that, because I had some measure of success, they would give me the recognition I deserved. But nope! They still didn't have anything good to say. After a few attempts to get them on board with no success, I quickly realized they were never going to be happy for me because they were jealous and toxic. As disappointing as this revelation was, it was something I just had to accept. You can't change people, and the quicker you realize this, the better.

Now, I keep them at arm's length; I don't allow my family members in my space for too long because they don't make me feel good. They drain my energy and contribute to my feelings of insecurity. Dealing with toxic family members is extremely difficult because they are your flesh and blood, and therefore we tend to be more lenient with them. We are quick to advise our loved ones to ditch a toxic romantic partner, but when it comes to family, we make excuses for them. Family is important when they are decent human beings. But when they are not, it is essential that you stay as far away from them as possible or they will have a negative effect on your mental health. Whether it's friends, family members, or co-workers, avoid toxic people at all costs.

Limit Negative Media: Between watching TV, reading newspapers, and scrolling through social media, you would never think that anything good happens in the world because we are bombarded with so much negativity. From wars, natural disasters, murders, and relationship dysfunction, bad news has become the norm. I was in the grocery store the other day, and while I waited in line to pay for my shopping, the people in front of me were talking about a recent bad event. How did they know about it? They had seen it on the news. The conversation was so exhausting that I had to try my best to tune it out. My point is that we are surrounded by negativity. If we don't see or read about the tragedies that are taking place in this world ourselves, someone will tell us about it.

Constant exposure to bad news leads to depression and anxiety because it can skew our perception of reality and give us a negativity bias. While it is true that the world can be a tremendously cruel place, there are also many wonderful things that happen all the time. Seeing bad news on daily basis can trigger stress responses in the body and cause chronic stress. You may not notice this immediately, but the emotional toll of processing distressing events can disrupt your emotional well-being, making it difficult for you to cope with your own life.

A positive environment is essential to developing confidence, and negative media content does not contribute to this. The constant exposure to bad news undermines your sense of security, making you feel hopeless and powerless. When you feel as if you don't have any control over your environment, you become overwhelmed with fear, which heightens your feelings of insecurity. To avoid being bombarded with negative media, do the following:

- **Use News Aggregators:** News aggregator apps and websites allow you to filter the type of news you see. For example, if you only want to know what's going on in politics, set the aggregator to receive political content only.

- **Set Boundaries:** One of the things I like about social media is that you can set boundaries. You can control what you see in your feed by blocking, unfollowing, and selecting "hide" for certain types of content. Only follow accounts that post inspirational, educational, or uplifting content. If you are not sure how to customize your feed, there are some very informative videos on YouTube that will teach you how to do this.

- **Mindful Consumption:** Pay attention to how you respond to the news. If you notice that certain stories or content cause a negative reaction, stop consuming that kind of content.

- **Seek Out Positive News:** Because the mainstream media focuses so heavily on sensationalism, you wouldn't think anything good ever happened in the world. But there are plenty of awesome things happening all the time, many of which are reported by positive media outlets. A quick Google search will pull them up. When I started watching positive media channels, I felt so much better. The stories make you smile and want to share them with friends and loved ones.

CREATE AN ALTER EGO

Who would believe that Beyoncé, one of the most successful female singers in the world, once lacked confidence when performing?

During an interview with *The Guardian*, Beyoncé stated that she had created an alter ego called Sasha Fierce to help her perform. Sasha was energetic, sexy, glamorous, and outspoken. When the time came for her to get on stage, she would put on her alternate personality. But seven years later, in an interview with *Allure* magazine, the popstar declared that Sasha Fierce was dead, and that she no longer needed her in order to be confident. Beyoncé faked it until she made it—and that is what confidence is all about. For most people, confidence doesn't come naturally and so a great way to develop it is to create an alter ego. Here are some tips on how to do this:

- **Decide:** Although you are creating an alter ego to develop confidence, what other goals do you want to accomplish with your alternate personality? Do you want to become a successful public speaker or businesswoman? Do you want to develop your personal brand? Write down all the reasons you want to create an alter ego.

- **Name/Personality:** Choose a name for your alter ego. Remember, it can be anything you want it to be because no one will know about it unless you decide to tell them. However, think about it carefully because there is power in a name. Going back to Beyoncé, *Sasha* means "defender, helper of mankind," and the dictionary definition of the word *fierce* is, "Having or displaying an intense or ferocious aggressiveness." To defend or to help mankind, you need to be extremely aggressive. Beyoncé knew that if she wanted to get to the top of her game, she needed to adopt that same level of aggressiveness. The personality of your alter ego is extremely important because that's what's going to carry you and make you appear confident. The personality of your alter ego should be based on your overall goal. For example, you are not going to choose a Sasha Fierce type character if you plan on becoming a public speaker. Instead, you might choose the personality of someone like Lisa Nichols who is a very successful motivational speaker. Or if you want to be more confident at social events, you can adopt a personality that is the opposite of yours. If you are shy and timid, become more brash and assertive.

Appearance: Is your alter ego flashy and out there, or more modest in appearance? The way your alter ego dresses should match their personality. But remember, the way you dress affects your confidence, so whatever appearance you choose, make sure you look the part.

- **Story:** Characters rarely exist in a vacuum; therefore, your alter ego should have a story to go alongside their personality and appearance. The story can be whatever you want it to be, whether it's remarkable or ordinary. Keeping the story vague makes it easier to remember. There is no right or wrong when it comes to creating a story for your alter ego—just make sure it's believable. Questions you can ask yourself when developing the story could include:
  - Where is your alter ego from?
  - What experiences have shaped them?
  - What kind of life have they lived?
  - What kind of people do they know?
  - What motivates them?

- **Get Into Character:** Now you have all the information about your alter ego, it's time to get into character. It's important to remember that you will only wear your alter ego when you want to achieve your goals. For instance, Beyoncé became Sasha Fierce before getting on stage. Most people who wear an alter ego drop the act before they arrive home or when they are around the people who truly know them. However, you will need to practice, so that switching between characters becomes second nature to you.

If you want more information about creating an alter ego, study people who have adopted one. They are more common than you may realize. Many celebrities and people in the public eye create alter egos to protect themselves from the criticism they receive from being in the media. Here are some of them:

- David Bowie – Ziggy Stardust
- Bono – MacPhisto
- Janelle Monae – Cindi Mayweather
- Prince – Camille
- Lady Gaga – Calderone

OVERCOME IMPOSTER SYNDROME

Imposter syndrome is when a person feels as if they don't belong in their position, no matter how hard they have worked for it. People can experience imposter syndrome in their career, romantic relationships, and friendships. It prevents you from developing confidence because you are always doubting yourself. Imposter syndrome is not considered a mental illness; it is typically connected to achievement and intelligence. The interesting thing about the syndrome is that people who suffer from it are often very successful. From the outside looking in, it makes no sense that they would feel this way, which is why it's so difficult to manage. But it is extremely common and makes people feel terribly insecure. Dr. Valerie Young did some research on imposter syndrome and found that there were five main types:

1. **The Expert:** No matter how intelligent you are, how many books you have read, or how many degrees you have earned, you will never know everything about a subject, and this is okay. But the expert feels that they have not quite reached the level of expert because they don't know everything, despite having secured a very high position in their field and being well-respected for their intellectual capabilities.

2. **The Perfectionist:** This type of imposter syndrome involves not believing you are good enough because you are not perfect. Other people are impressed by your abilities, but you don't think you deserve it.

3. **The Super Person:** The super person believes they must be the best at everything; if not, they are a fraud.

4. **The Soloist:** Hard work paves the way to success. However, it is not uncommon for people to become successful because they met someone in a position of power. Soloists believe that if they didn't get to the top by themselves, they don't deserve to be in the position they are in.

5. **The Natural Genius:** The natural genius believes they are an imposter if they have had to learn a particular skill. According to them, if something doesn't come naturally to them, it means they are not really good at it.

THE CAUSES OF IMPOSTER SYNDROME

Research suggests that the root causes of imposter syndrome are the way children were raised and gender dynamics. It does not affect certain groups of people more than others. Studies have found that approximately seventy percent of people will experience imposter syndrome at least once in their lives. Here are some of the main causes of imposter syndrome:

Upbringing: Overprotective and controlling parenting styles can trigger imposter syndrome. Parents who put pressure on their children to be high achievers or who praise their children one minute and criticize them the next are also responsible for causing imposter syndrome. Additionally, studies suggest that children raised in conflict-ridden homes with unsupportive parents may experience imposter syndrome as adults.

New Opportunities: New opportunities such as starting college or a new job can cause people to feel as if they don't belong there. The new environment with all the new social rules to learn can have you feeling as if you shouldn't be there and that you are incapable of performing effectively. Trying something new or going through a major life change can trigger imposter syndrome because you may feel pressured to achieve a high standard that you don't think you can meet.

Personality: Some personality traits are more prone to imposter syndrome than others. These include:

- **Neuroticism:** Neurotic people experience high levels of insecurity, anxiety, guilt, and tension. These feelings can make them feel like an imposter when in certain environments.

- **Low Self-Efficacy:** When a person doesn't believe in their ability to succeed, they are more likely to suffer from imposter syndrome.

- **Highly Sensitive:** Highly sensitive people are prone to imposter syndrome because of their sensitive nature. Their feelings of insecurity regarding their capabilities on a job or in a relationship are intensified, which can cause them to feel like a fraud.

Social Anxiety: Social anxiety and imposter syndrome are similar but they are not the same. Social anxiety disorder causes a person to feel uncomfortable in social situations. They feel as if they don't fit in when in a conversation with someone; or when they are doing something like giving a speech in front of an audience, they become fearful that people will realize they don't belong there.

The symptoms associated with social anxiety can feed imposter syndrome; however, not everyone with imposter syndrome suffers from social anxiety, and vice versa. Imposter syndrome can cause anxiety when a person is in a situation in which they don't feel they deserve to be.

Signs That You Have Imposter Syndrome

As mentioned, the majority of people experience imposter syndrome at some point in their life. Here are some of the main signs:

- **Downplaying Expertise:** Feeling that you don't deserve to have such a high position because you are not really an expert. You believe you don't know enough to consider yourself an expert.

- **Fear of Being Exposed:** You live in constant fear that people will discover you are a fraud and that you are not really that great after all.

- **Comparison:** You are always comparing yourself to people and feeling that they are more intelligent, successful, or talented than you.

- **Avoiding Attention:** Anything that attracts praise and recognition, you avoid. You don't want the spotlight on you because you are afraid people will discover you are a fraud.

- **Perfectionism:** Setting such high standards for yourself that it is impossible to meet them. When you don't meet the standards you set for yourself, you get upset.

- **Undermining Achievement:** Despite the fact that everything you do is sprinkled with excellence, you are constantly downplaying your achievements, referring to them as "no big deal," or claiming that anyone could have done the same.

- **Overworking:** You overwork yourself because you are afraid people are going to find out that you are not really as great as they think you are.

- **Fear of Failure:** You are terrified of making mistakes, so you procrastinate and never get started on projects, to avoid failure.

- **Self-Doubt:** You are always questioning whether you are good enough. You feel unsure about your talents and skills, despite the evidence confirming that you are in fact brilliant.

- **Discrediting Your Success:** When you do well at something, you believe it's because you got lucky and not because of your hard work and natural abilities.

How to Overcome Imposter Syndrome

To overcome imposter syndrome, start by asking yourself these difficult questions:

- In my current state, do I believe I deserve love?
- Do I need to be perfect to get the approval of others?
- What belief systems do I hold about myself?

To liberate yourself from the negative feelings associated with imposter syndrome, you need to challenge these unhealthy beliefs that have become a normal part of your existence. You will find answering these questions painful because you may not even be aware of the fact that you hold these beliefs. Because they are at work within your subconscious mind, they guide your behavior and you have never questioned them until now. Now you have insight into how you truly feel about yourself, it's time to eliminate these feelings.

Focus on Facts: Although your feelings are important and valid, when it comes to imposter syndrome, your feelings are destructive. They will cause you to ignore the reality of your situation and lead you in the wrong direction. The problem with feelings is that they are temporary. When you walk into a room full of important people and feel as if you don't belong there, that feeling isn't going to last. However, the actions you take because of those feelings can change the trajectory of your destiny. For example, your feelings of inadequacy cause you to reject a job interview because you don't believe you are capable of doing the job. You threw away a once-in-a-life-time opportunity because of how you felt. But the facts are that the person who offered you the interview had faith in your abilities and felt that you would be an asset to their company. Here are some tips on how to focus on the facts and not your feelings:

- **Acknowledge Your Feelings:** As mentioned, your feelings are valid and you are entitled to feel how you feel. However, regardless of the situation, it's important not to allow your feelings to dictate your actions. This is the first step in helping you detach your emotions from the facts of the situation.

- **Gather Evidence:** When you start feeling like you are not good enough, what evidence do you have to support how you feel? Remember, in a court of law, evidence is not about how you feel or what you suspect. A lawyer needs to present facts to the jury to convince them to make a decision. What factual evidence do you have to support your feelings? If you don't have any, you can conclude that they are incorrect.

- **Use Logical Reasoning:** To separate your facts from your feelings, keep your mind fixed on objective information by applying logical reasoning and critical thinking to evaluate the information.

- **Examine Different Perspectives:** Gain a thorough view of the situation by evaluating it from different angles. This helps to prevent personal bias and stops your emotions from clouding your judgment.

- **Seek Feedback:** Ask the people you trust for their opinion about your conclusions. Let's say you've been asked to lead an important project at work but you're telling yourself you won't be able to take on the role because you are not smart enough. You can start by asking your manager why they chose you for the task, and then ask friends and family what they think. You will often find that people see you differently to the way you see yourself.

Talk About It: Living with imposter syndrome is stressful, and one way to relieve stress is to talk about your problems. Studies have found that sharing our negative emotions with someone we trust promotes healing by reducing emotional distress. Self-disclosure is a form of release; when you keep your problems to yourself, they get worse because you keep thinking about them. The next time imposter syndrome attempts to hijack your brain, call a friend. You will quickly find that sharing your thoughts makes it a lot easier to overcome imposter syndrome.

Get Off Social Media: One of the things that people with imposter syndrome struggle with is comparing themselves to others. A study conducted by Florida House Experience found that sixty-five percent of men and eighty-seven percent of women compared their bodies to the images they saw on social media. While this study was about physical appearance, what it highlighted was that social media makes people insecure because they are constantly comparing themselves with the supposed perfect lives of influencers and celebrities. While there are many benefits to social media, it can also be extremely destructive, and if you are not strong enough to protect yourself against its poison, it will destroy your life. Unfortunately, getting off social media is easier said than done because it's addictive and most people are unaware they are addicted to it. Basically, if you can't go half an hour without checking Instagram, you're hooked. Does this sound like you? Don't worry, we've all been there. I was addicted to social media too a few years back, but I kicked the habit by doing a digital detox for thirty days.

I'm not going to delve deep into the science of why social media is addictive, but what you need to do is reset your dopamine levels. The problem with today's society is that we are constantly staring at a screen and bombarded with new information every few seconds. For a lot of us, this information is exciting, whether it's the latest celebrity gossip, a post from our favorite influencer, or insight into the lives of our loved ones. The little red notification signals cause a surge of the feel-good hormone dopamine to rush through our brain. The more we engage with online content, the more we want of it. Social media addicts chase the high in the same way drug addicts do. The more they use drugs, the more they need, because the high isn't as good as the first one. Social media is no different. Social media is like a deep, dark tunnel that people get lost in and can't seem to find their way out of. For highly sensitive people and empaths, the dangers of social media are even worse. It makes them more depressed, anxious, and stressed out than the average person.

Drug addicts go to rehab to reset their dopamine levels. The more time they spend not using, the less they desire the drug because there is no high to trigger the release of dopamine. The same is true of social media addicts. By unplugging for thirty days, your desire to scroll will decrease and you will overcome the habit of picking up your phone every few minutes. The key is to replace a bad habit with a good one. What worked for me was to keep a book with me at all times. Whenever I felt the urge to pick up my phone, I would pick up my book and read a few pages. It was hard at first, but it slowly became very rewarding. I was no longer filling my head with garbage and feeling insecure because I didn't look like an Instagram model. Social media had stolen my mind. I took it back—and I would advise you to do the same.

Today, I can take it or leave it. I will scroll every once in a while, but my mind has been deprogrammed. Once you realize that the people you were so envious of are just normal human beings with everyday issues, you stop obsessing over them. Social media is not real life; the celebrities and influencers show you only the positive aspects of their lives. You won't find them posting about the struggles of life because they won't get any likes, comments, and views. They are forced to present a false narrative because that's what everyone wants to see. As far as I'm concerned, it's a form of escapism. People are so fed up with their lives that they live vicariously through the lives of the rich and famous, hoping it will make them feel better—but it just makes them feel worse.

Celebrate Your Wins: Get used to congratulating yourself for your success, even if it's something small. The practice of celebrating your wins reminds you that you are responsible for your success. Whatever you achieved wasn't a fluke and nor was it an accident. You don't need to have a huge celebration to celebrate your wins; a small treat like ordering your favorite takeout, or watching an entire season of your favorite show on Netflix will suffice. As long as you know that you are celebrating your wins, that's all that matters.

Ditch Perfectionism: I am a firm believer in doing everything with excellence. However, perfection doesn't exist so there is no point in trying to attain it. The reason I can say with confidence that perfectionism doesn't exist is that the definition of perfect is relative. What's perfect to you might not be perfect to someone else. Let me give you an example. When I was doing my master's degree, my final project was to write a dissertation. There were two markers for the project. My supervisor thought my work was excellent and gave me an A, but the second marker thought it was a load of trash and gave it a C. During their discussion about their marking discrepancy, they both put forward their arguments about the reasons for their grades. Same paper; two completely different opinions. They met in the middle and I ended up with a B, but my point is that they didn't agree. Have you ever heard the saying, "One man's trash is another man's treasure?" Whatever you work on, do your best, but don't stress over perfection or you will never get it done.

Say Yes: People with imposter syndrome do everything in their power to avoid accepting new opportunities because they are afraid they will be exposed as a fraud. You can't take on everything you are offered or you will become overwhelmed and stressed out—but you *can* accept some opportunities. Only turn down opportunities if you've got too many things on your plate. But if you can take on a new challenge, do it, because you don't know what doors could open for you. The next time you're about to decline an opportunity, remember what Richard Branson said: "If someone offers you an amazing opportunity and you are not sure you can do it, say yes. Then learn how to do it later."

As someone who suffers from imposter syndrome, it's definitely going to be hard taking on roles you're not confident about. But just remember that the person who gave you the opportunity did so because they believed you were capable of doing it. If someone else can believe in you, why can't you believe in yourself?

It's important to mention that it will take a lot of work to overcome imposter syndrome. However, if you are consistent and keep applying the above strategies, you will slowly begin to eradicate these negative feelings from your life.

At the beginning of the chapter, I said that we are born with confidence, but by the time we are about five years old, we lose it.

Now you have reclaimed your confidence, and you understand that your environment, people, and the things you consume can contribute to how you feel about yourself, do everything in your power to ensure that your confidence is never stolen from you again.

Most people live to die. Sad but true. They work in a job they can't stand, pay bills, retire, and go to the grave. What a tragedy. It is rare that you hear of people doing anything of substance because the average person lives in survival mode and they don't have time to even consider doing anything other than keep a roof over their heads and their children fed. But I believe there is more to life than this. If you truly desire to live a fulfilling life, finding your purpose is the first step. Keep reading to discover how you can start living a purpose-driven life today.

CHAPTER 4:

DEFINING YOUR LEGACY: YOU HAVE A PURPOSE

L iving an exceptional life is not relegated to a few lucky people. Everyone is born with the ability to leave a unique and lasting impact on the world. However, living a purpose-driven life is not something we are encouraged to do. For most of us, from the day we are born, we are groomed to get an education and find a career. While it is important to make a good living for yourself, your number one priority should be to find your true purpose. Not doing what you were destined to makes life meaningless. It is not uncommon for people to ask themselves, "What is the purpose of life?" because deep down, they know there is more to life than what they are experiencing.

Leaving a legacy is about more than giving your children an inheritance when you die; it's the lasting influence of your actions, values, and relationships. Defining your legacy starts with gaining a deep understanding of who you are and what you stand for. When you are clear about your purpose here on Earth, it provides you with motivation and direction. Your days become filled with purpose-driven activities because now, your life has meaning. Oscar Wilde once said, "To live is the rarest thing in the world, because most people just exist and that's all." If you are tired of just existing, and you want to start living, this chapter is for you.

WHAT LEGACY DO YOU WANT TO LEAVE?

Several years ago, my mentor gave me the most profound task I have ever carried out in my life. It touched my soul in a way that I don't even have the words to articulate. My mentor's name is Jackie, and she told me to write my own eulogy. When she initially mentioned it, I looked at her as if she had completely lost her mind. But after she explained it, my mind was blown. Jackie turned her life around after her husband died in a car accident. He kissed her goodbye in the morning, and the next time she saw him was two hours later as she identified his body in the mortuary. After many months of depression, she came to the conclusion that not only was life too short to remain depressed; it was too short not to live a meaningful and accomplished life.

Jackie loved her husband immensely. According to her, he was a phenomenal man. However, he did not live the life he dreamed about. He talked about it a lot, but he didn't live it, and when he died, that was one of the most heartbreaking things Jackie dealt with—the thought that his life was never truly *lived*. Jackie wrote his eulogy for his funeral, and then several months later, she wrote another one, for the life she knew he had truly wanted to live. She keeps that eulogy on her desk and reads it every morning.

When Jackie told me to write my eulogy, she gave several instructions: to imagine that I had lived to the ripe old age of one hundred; to decide how I wanted my loved ones to remember me; to imagine that I had achieved every single last one of my dreams; and to let everyone know how important it was to find their purpose and live it to the fullest. The point of writing my eulogy was so I could determine my legacy. It was a very powerful assignment. But Jackie also wanted me to think about something we never think about until it happens, and that is death. One thing in life that is certain is that we are all going to die one day, though we don't know when that day is going to be. She said I should live every day like it was my last because you never know when you will take your last breath. While writing my eulogy, I added a date for my future death. At the top of the Word document, there were two dates: the day I was born, and the day I died. I then began to think how differently I would have lived my life up until that point if when we were born, we were given a birth and a death certificate. If we all knew what date we were going to die, we would stop being so reckless with our lives. But because we don't know, we have created this false reality for ourselves. I have learned that those who think about death invest time in living. To determine what legacy you want to leave, write your eulogy.

Step 1: Imagine you have reached the ripe old age of one hundred years old and you have achieved all your dreams. Reflect on your life experiences and the relationships that have been the most important to you. Consider the things that you value the most and how you want people to remember you.

Step 2: Decide what you will focus on the most. This could include the impact you have had on others, your values, passions, accomplishments. You might want to include some common themes such as personal growth, perseverance, love, or service to others.

Step 3: What stories and anecdotes do you want to use for the focus points in step 2? Think about important moments in your life that emphasize your character and the way you lived.

Step 4: Think about the people who will be at your funeral. What are the things that are important to them? What are the main messages you want them to take away from your eulogy?

Step 5: Now you have all the information to get started with your eulogy, start writing a draft. It should contain an introduction where you set the tone and introduce the main themes. The body is where you expand on those themes. Close with a powerful statement that sums up your message and captures the heart of the guests at your funeral.

Step 6: Your eulogy should be authentic and reflect your personality and voice.

Step 7: If you trust anyone enough to share your eulogy with them, explain why you wrote it and get some feedback.

WHY PURPOSE IS IMPORTANT

A study conducted by researcher Kaylin Ratner found that people who lived purpose-driven lives were happier. They felt more positive emotions such as joy, enthusiasm, and contentment. Additionally, they felt less sad, angry, anxious, and sluggish. They were more satisfied with life and they were hopeful for the future. Many more studies agree with Ratner's findings, and have also discovered that purpose has several benefits including reduced feelings of loneliness, less cardiovascular disease, and less death. Also, companies who focus on purpose are more successful. Employees for these companies are happier, find work to be more meaningful, and are more productive.

Unfortunately, many people drift through life without finding their real purpose. There are many reasons for this, but one of them is a skewed understanding of purpose. The assumption is that purpose is about working to resolve gigantic problems like poverty and world peace. While these are worthwhile endeavors, and I am eternally grateful to the people who have dedicated their lives to these causes, they are not the only things you can do to live out your purpose. It is important to understand that whatever contribution you make to the world with your skills and talents is related to your purpose. Your significance might come from the work you do for your friends, family, community, or team. The kind of work you do is irrelevant—as long as it is meaningful to you, that's all that matters. There are several reasons why purpose is so important. Here are some of them:

Focus: The moment I realized I had a life's purpose and I started working towards it, I began leaping out of bed every morning. Prior to that, I hit the snooze button until I had minutes to spare and dragged myself to the shower. Opening my eyes was literal torture because I hated every aspect of my life. Knowing that I had to work in a job I detested for eight hours a day was gut-wrenching. Each week, I counted down the days until Friday and then drowned my sorrows until Monday. Apparently, I wasn't the only person who hated their job, because according to a global poll conducted by Gallup, an astonishing eighty-five percent of people hate their jobs. So, why are they there? Because they've got bills to pay and families to look after—it's as simple as that.

When I wasn't working, my days were filled with nothingness. Going out with friends, and doing random, meaningless things for the most part was just about as boring as going to work (although I loved my friends). I wasted so much time watching endless hours of TV, scrolling, talking on the phone, window shopping or just staring into space. As far as I was concerned, life was pointless. Days turned into weeks, weeks turned into months, and months turned into years. Year after year, I became ever more dissatisfied with life. But when I started my self-development journey and realized I had a purpose, life took on a whole new meaning. As mentioned, I started leaping out of bed in the mornings, I had a goal to work towards, my days were planned, and I became completely focused on writing my first book. It was a glorious feeling.

Without something to focus on, you become like a ship at sea being tossed to and fro by the waves. You have no stability, and nothing to anchor you during times of trouble—because, trust and do believe, trouble is going to come. I talked about this in Chapter 1. However, when trouble *does* come, the fact that you know you have something important to do with your life will keep you grounded. Your purpose will stop you from wasting time because it will keep you so consumed that you won't have time to waste. The scrolling, the phone calls, the mindless watching of TV will stop when life has meaning.

Connection: It is not uncommon for people to feel disconnected from society. This disconnection can quickly lead to anxiety, depression, and other mental health challenges. But when your work is important to others, you feel a great sense of joy and pride. When you know that what you do makes the lives of others better, it motivates you to want to continue. Again, please understand that when I say, "Your work is important to others," I don't mean you are necessarily out there saving the world. Whatever skill or talent you have that benefits others is what I mean. I have a friend (let's call her Fran) who suffers from alopecia and has to wear wigs. She has a personal wig maker who comes to her house and fits and styles her wigs. It is Fran's greatest joy that not only does she have access to realistic-looking hair, but the hairdresser comes to her house to fit it. Fran doesn't feel comfortable going out in public with her bald head, so going to a salon is out of the question for her. She used to buy wigs online and fit them herself because she refused to go to a packed salon. But because she isn't an expert, with all due respect, her wigs were not realistic-looking, and so she wore scarfs or hats over them to make them more believable. Fran's wig maker is living her purpose and using her skills to make the lives of others better.

The other day, I went to the store to buy some new forks and tomato purée. There were two floors in the store. The home-equipment part was upstairs, so I went looking for some forks. I walked up and down the aisles and couldn't find them. I saw a customer service assistant and asked her where the forks were, and she walked me right to them. I was so grateful. When I went downstairs looking for the tomato purée, I couldn't find that either, but there was no one around to ask, so, like before, I walked up and down the aisles searching. I was wandering around like a headless chicken until I bumped into the same customer service assistant from upstairs. I asked her where the tomato purée was, and she walked me right to it. I didn't just say "thank you" and keep it moving. I told her how grateful I was for her assistance because I had somewhere to go and didn't have time to spend the whole day looking for items. She made my life a lot easier. I asked for her name (it was Alison), and wrote a good review about my experience. Customer service jobs are often looked down upon because employees are paid minimum wage. But what would we do if there were no customer service assistants? To start, there would be no stores for us to shop in. I don't know whether Alison was happy with her job, but what I do know is that she was good at it. She walked me right to the forks and the tomato purée without a second's hesitation, which means one of her skills is that she has a good memory. It may not be Alison's life purpose to work as a customer service assistant, but whether she knew it or not, she had found purpose in her job with how excellent she was at helping people.

Motivation: Motivation is essential if you are going to achieve your goals. But the problem with motivation is that it's just like any other emotion—it's temporary. Have you ever watched a motivational film, listened to a speech, or read a book and felt a surge of motivation to get stuff done? Whether it was to go to the gym, start a business, or improve your diet, you were raring to go. But after a few days of taking action, that motivation disappeared and you returned to your old ways of hitting the snooze button, making excuses, and saying you will do it tomorrow, but tomorrow never comes. There are two types of motivation: intrinsic and extrinsic.

- **Intrinsic Motivation:** Intrinsic motivation is when we do things because they make us happy. Your motivation to participate in the activity comes from within, and not because of an external reward.

- **Extrinsic Motivation:** Extrinsic motivation is driven by external rewards such as money, fame, or praise. Basically, it's when people do things not because they have a deep desire to do it, but because they are going to get something out of it.

If you hate your job, you are extrinsically motivated to go to work every day because you need the money. You will be surprised that some famous people hate being famous, but whether it's acting or singing, they do it for the money. Some people are amazed when a person working in a high-paid job quits for a job that pays way less money. From the outside looking in, it seems that the individual has downgraded their job. But the person who took the pay cut did it because they hated their job and only went to work for the money. Their new job is something that fulfils them and that they actually want to do (intrinsic motivation). They no longer wake up dreading having to go to work.

Having a purpose gives you intrinsic motivation. You now have a strong desire to do work for no other reason than you love what you do. The motivation you now have continuously pushes you to make a positive impact on the lives of those around you and to strive for excellence.

How to Find Your Purpose

I wrote about purpose briefly in Chapter 2. I am now going to go into it in more depth. Here's a quick recap. Your purpose is about what you were created to do, and once you find that, you will find true joy and fulfilment. The question I am often asked is *how do you find your purpose?* I believe there are several routes to discovering your purpose, but there is also a specific process you can follow to find it. The process is what I am going to focus on in this section.

Your Purpose Is a Journey: Research suggests that one in three retirees say they feel depressed after retirement. That's because they no longer have direction and routine in their lives. They went from going to work Monday to Friday, to staying at home all day with nothing to do. The retirees who get depressed had a job; they didn't have a purpose. When you have a purpose, there is no retirement— you keep doing what you are doing until the day you die. My friend Sandy's mother was a health visitor. She chose that profession because she is passionate about making sure the marginalized have access to decent healthcare. Her job involved visiting families with children up to the age of five and conducting assessments to identify health needs. She had a keen eye for early signs of sickness and saved a lot of lives because she was able to spot illnesses before they got any worse. Her job was her pride and joy, but it was also her purpose, and when she retired, she joined a volunteer agency and continued her work as a health visitor. At seventy-six years old, Sandy's mother goes out for three hours per day Monday to Friday to check on the health of young children. Once a year she travels to Africa to do the same. She is a very joyful and energetic woman, and she has vowed not to stop working until the day she dies. I am very proud of her.

When I say that your purpose is a journey and not a destination, I mean that your travels will be continuous; you won't get off the ride of life until you die. There is no retirement or endpoint when it comes to purpose. You will keep growing, evolving, discovering, and contributing to your community. You will gather an abundance of experiences and learn many lessons along the way. Every challenge you encounter will contribute to shaping your purpose. Viewing your purpose as a journey encourages you to see the value in the present moment instead of focusing on long-term goals. It will allow you to appreciate the process of becoming who you were destined to become. This journey-focused view of purpose helps to build resilience. When purpose is seen as a destination, failures and setbacks can become overwhelming because it seems as if we are being pushed further and further away from our goals. But when we view purpose as a journey, these hindrances are seen as an important part of the process. They are opportunities for learning and growth. This perspective motivates you to keep going even when things are not working out as planned. When you understand that every experience, whether positive or negative, contributes to your journey, the road becomes a lot easier to travel.

WHAT ARE YOUR VALUES?

Your values are your priorities; they are the things you believe are the most important in your life. They are like a guiding force and help you make decisions such as your career choice, and the person you desire to marry. Most people have never actually thought about their values, so here are some questions to help you clarify them:

- If I could make one change right now to make the world a better place, what would it be?

- What type of world do I desire to live in?

- What is the most important characteristic a person should have?

- If you have children, what values are you instilling in them? If you plan on having children, what values will you instill in them?

- What has been the most memorable experience of your life and why?

- If you were left an inheritance of $100 million, what would you do with the money?

- Who in your life do you admire the most, and what three qualities do you admire about them?

- If you were on your deathbed right now, what would you regret not doing?

- What does freedom look like to you?

- What are you the most proud of about yourself?

What Are Your Passions?

Your passions are the things you love that light a fire in you. When you are working on your passions, you get completely submerged in them and lose track of time. The closest people to you will know what your passions are because you are always talking about them. I believe that everyone is passionate about something. If you are not sure what you are passionate about, here are some questions to ask yourself:

- What did you enjoy doing the most as a child?

- What do you enjoy talking about extensively?

- If you had complete financial freedom, what would you be doing?

- What is the most fulfilling thing in your life right now?

- What are the things you daydream about?

- What are the things that bring you the most joy?

- What do you want to learn more about?

- What is working well in your life right now and why?

- What is the one thing you would like to do before you die?

- Are there any common themes in your life?

What Are Your Strengths?

Your strengths are not only about your talents and skills. Your strengths are a combination of qualities, traits, and abilities that define how you show up in the world. Your strengths are revealed in your platonic and romantic relationships, and in your job. Basically, the people you spend the most time with know what your strengths are. Here are some questions to ask yourself to identify your strengths:

- What tasks or activities can you perform with ease?

- What do the people closest to you compliment you about the most?

- What qualities do you have that help you deal with challenges?

- What roles do you thrive in the most?

- What do your managers say about you at your performance reviews?

- What would you say you can do better than most people?

- What things do you find extremely satisfying?

- When are you the most self-disciplined?

- What type of advice do your friends ask you for the most?

- If you were asked to complete a difficult task, what characteristics do you possess that would help you to complete it?

Now you have answered these questions, you should have a clear sense of your purpose. But one last thing I want to say is that sometimes your purpose is born out of your pain. There are some people who have experienced terrible tragedies but these have inspired them to do great things. One of my heroes is the late Nelson Mandela. He spent twenty-seven years in prison for crimes he didn't commit and went on to become the first black president of South Africa. Sometimes, adversity paves the way to destiny, and it must happen like that because, for some people, their destiny is so great that they need to be extremely resilient to walk in it. Adversity builds resilience in a way that nothing else can. Writer and poet Khalil Gibran once said, "Out of suffering have emerged the strongest souls; the most massive characters are seared with scars." Think about it like this: human beings don't like suffering. Society promotes it as the worst possible thing that can happen to you, and so people avoid it at all costs. We are in the constant pursuit of happiness. If you were given a book of your life at the age of thirteen and it told you exactly how your life was going to turn out and it was full of suffering, you would choose a different path. Let's use Nelson Mandela as an example. His book said he would spend twenty-seven years in prison, during which time he would be isolated for the first eighteen years and denied visits from friends and family. He wouldn't sleep on a bed, but on a cold stone floor, and his days would be spent doing hard labor. After he had been through all this hardship, he would enjoy the best years of his life as the first president of South Africa. Had Nelson Mandela known this beforehand, I am almost certain he would have declined the destiny he was presented with.

The universe has an interesting way of getting us where we need to be in life, and sometimes, it is through excruciating pain.

How to Start Living Your Purpose

For many people, once they know what their purpose is, they hit a brick wall. It's like, "Now what? I've got all this information—what do I do with it?" Let me start by saying that, although living your purpose is the most fulfilling thing you will ever do, it is also the most difficult. There will be many obstacles and setbacks along the way. Unfortunately, this is where most people give up. They assume that if there are so many roadblocks, they cannot be heading in the right direction. This is a genuine question, and it makes logical sense, but it's important that you understand how the universe works. Think of the universe as a loving parent who wants their child to have the best in life. So, when their son/daughter asks them for something really expensive, a responsible parent isn't going to give it to them immediately because then the child will assume they can get whatever they want when they want and ignore the fact that there are rules to the game. Instead, the parents will agree to the gift, but only after the child has worked for it. They might require the child to get good grades throughout the year, or contribute to the gift by doing extra chores around the house for money. If the child is serious about what they want, they will do the work required to get it.

The universe works in the same way; it will test you to ensure you really want what you say you want. This test will happen in several ways. First, are you willing to prepare for your purpose? You might need to get certified, or go back to school to get a specific qualification. When you think you are ready, and that it's time to start walking in your purpose, all hell will break lose. This phenomenon is referred to as Murphy's Law. It's when everything that could go wrong will go wrong. What do you do when you run into obstacle after obstacle? Keep pushing, or give up? Unfortunately, at this point, most people give up—and the statistics prove it. Research suggests that forty-five percent of small businesses fail within the first five years. I can't find any statistics stating that these same business owners try again. It is rare that people keep trying after failure. I believe that's because the majority of people don't understand that failure is a part of success. In my personal experience, based on the successful people I know and the successful people I've studied, you learn more from failure than you do from success.

One of my favorite success stories is about Les Brown, one of the most successful motivational speakers in the world. He went through many failures while trying to live out his purpose. He became homeless and slept in his office. When his speaker's career started taking off and he managed to buy a house for his mother, he lost it because there was a debt attached to the house that he wasn't aware of before purchasing it. He was forced to move out of the house thirty days after buying it. Les Brown invested every penny into that house and was left without a cent to his name. He moved back into his mother's old home—the one he moved her out of—and had to start building from scratch. He had many more trials along the way, but still managed to become one of the best motivational speakers in the world. Les Brown has inspired millions of people and helped to transform their lives. Had he given up at the first hurdle, the world would have been robbed of his gift. Are you willing to walk through the fire to live out your purpose? If you answered yes to this question, keep reading.

Step Outside Your Comfort Zone: It is human nature to want remain in our comfort zone because it keeps us alive, and it's predictable. Stepping outside of your comfort zone goes against human nature. However, if you are serious about becoming the person you know you were destined to become, it is essential that you learn to become comfortable with being uncomfortable, because that is how you grow and learn. The person who desires to transform their body understands this. They keep lifting heavier weights to put pressure on the muscles because without pressure, the muscles won't grow. The next morning, the body is sore, and the last thing you want to do is get out of bed and go to the gym again. But that's how you know the weight lifting is working—because you feel the pain. Here are some tips on how to step outside your comfort zone:

- **Confront Your Fears:** If you are not ready to confront your fears, you are not ready to live a purpose-driven life. My worst fear has always been public speaking. I didn't like it five years ago, and I don't like it now. If I was ever chosen to give a speech at an event, or a presentation at work, I found a way out of it. I was determined that I would never speak in front of an audience. My fear was that I would mess up, forget what I was saying, or trip up on my words. I didn't want to deal with the embarrassment of messing up, so I avoided it altogether. The interesting thing about confronting your fears is that once you confront them, the experience is never as bad as you had envisioned it to be. The acronym for the word *fear* is *False Evidence Appearing Real.* When we are afraid of something, our mind plays tricks on us, and we begin to imagine everything that could go wrong. We spend so much time thinking about it that we convince ourselves it's real. Whatever fears you have are valid; however, the thoughts running around in your head about your fears are not real. After challenging myself to speak in public, although I was definitely nervous, all the things I had convinced myself were going to happen, didn't happen. As mentioned, I still don't like public speaking, and it still makes me nervous, but I do it anyway because it's how I challenge myself.

- **Associate With Experts:** Friend groups are typically all on the same level. You will rarely come across a group of friends where there are large disparities between them. For example, they usually earn a similar amount of money, they are all the same race, or share a similar level of attractiveness. Experts refer to this phenomenon as "social identity —

theory," which states that we prefer being around people who are similar to us because it helps us construct our identity. On the other hand, associating with people who are different to us can make us feel very uncomfortable. I remember the first time I met up with my mentor Jackie; she arrived in a Jaguar, and I drove a beat-up Toyota! I was embarrassed and in awe all at the same time. It was very intimidating being in the presence of someone so powerful.

I remember lying in bed that night feeling terribly insecure, wondering whether I would ever become as successful as her. But being around her inspired me to work on myself because she gave me insight into what life can become if you do the work. The problem with associating with people who are similar to you is they don't challenge you to do better because in most cases, they are comfortable where they are. When someone in the group decides to elevate, it causes friction. That's exactly what happened to me (I will discuss that in Chapter 7). Motivational speaker Jim Rohn once said, "You become the average of the people you spend the most time with." And author Dennis Kimbro said, "If you are the smartest person in your group, you need to find a new group." Both of these quotes encourage us to step out of our comfort zone if we want to change. If you examine the lives of the people you spend the most time with and determine that you don't want to be like them ten years from now, it's time to leave the group. And if you are the smartest person in your friend group, you will never grow, because you won't feel the need to.

- **Take Risks:** Playing it safe won't get you anywhere in life, but unfortunately, that's what we've been conditioned to do: get an education and find a job that will give you a good pension when you retire. All your bills will be paid every month, and you might have a little extra to do a few nice things like go on vacation. People who take risks to accomplish their goals are seen as rebels and are chastised for it. Take Tyler Perry, for example. He is a filmmaker, playwright, and the owner of the Tyler Perry Studios, built on a three-hundred-acre lot. When he first started making films, he ended up homeless. He started writing films in the early 1990s and didn't get a major breakthrough until 2005. His mother got so tired of him always asking for money and, as far as she was concerned, living in fantasy land about becoming a filmmaker that she told him to go and get a job at the local phone company because they provided good benefits. His mother couldn't see his vision and wanted him to play it safe. That's how the majority of people think.

Successful people don't play it safe because to them, there is no such thing as failure. If it doesn't work out, it wasn't meant to be—they learn from it and keep it moving. Risk takers live on the edge; if they are passionate about something, they go for it, and they don't allow anyone or anything to stop them.

Bill Gates was a student at Harvard, one of the most prestigious universities in the United States. But he had a dream to start a computer company and he dropped out of college to pursue it. I am sure many people didn't agree with his decision, but it paid off in the end because, according to *Forbes* magazine, he is the ninth richest person in the world.

Beyoncé was once a member of the musical girl group Destiny's Child. They were extremely successful as a group, but how were things going to work out for her as a solo artist? She had no idea, but she did it anyway. Today, with thirty-two Grammys, and eighty-eight Grammy nominations, Beyoncé has won more Grammys than any other artist in history. She took a huge risk by going solo, and it paid off.

Sylvester Stallone didn't have a penny to his name when he wrote the film *Rocky*. Producers offered him big money to turn the script into a film, but he saw himself as the lead role and refused the offers unless they gave it to him. Although Stallone had starred in several films, he wasn't well known and was basically still a starving actor. The producers wanted a successful actor to play the role. However, he stood his ground, and eventually they agreed. *Rocky* was the most successful film of 1976. Sylvester Stallone went on to become one of the most successful actors of all time.

If you are not used to taking risks, relinquish your fears and start taking them. You don't need to do anything wild—start small and work your way up. For example, go and invite the hot guy you've been crushing on at work out for a coffee. The worst that can happen is that he will say no. The best that can happen is that he says yes, and you end up dating. You will never know if you don't try. Had Bill Gates, Beyoncé, and Sylvester Stallone not taken a risk, they would not be the successful people they are today.

Try New Things: What have you always wanted to do that you haven't done yet? Or that you are afraid to do? Mine was solo travel. Every year, I went on vacation with my girls, but when those friendships collapsed, I thought it would be the perfect opportunity to travel alone. I had always wanted to travel solo but I was afraid. I wasn't just scared of being a lone female in a foreign country; I was concerned about things like eating alone, and talking to strangers. But I plucked up the courage to do it and traveled to Australia. It was one of the best decisions of my life! I found it helpful to write a bucket list of one hundred things I wanted to do before I died. I am currently halfway through that list, and it feels amazing to keep ticking them off one by one.

Volunteer: Whatever it is you want to do, you will need experience—and a great way to get some is by volunteering. To help take my writing to the next level, I volunteered to write for a local magazine for one year and it was extremely helpful. I believed I was a good writer until my work got edited by real editors. I quickly learned that my grammar was terrible, I overused words, and my sentences were long-winded! I wasn't feeling the constructive criticism at all, and after my first submission, I wanted to quit. But I couldn't allow pride to get in the way of this opportunity. I had applied to volunteer for several magazines and newspapers and got rejected by every last one of them except the one I was writing for. I knew I had hit the jackpot and I needed to see it through. I am so glad I did because not only did I learn a lot and improve my writing skills tremendously, but up until this day, they promote my books for free in their magazine and on their social media pages!

Whatever it is you want to do, send some emails to a few companies and see if you can get your foot in the door. It might take a while to get a response, but don't let that discourage you. Once you get a volunteer position, do your best work—you never know what opportunities could come out of it. Motivational speaker Les Brown once told a story about a man who lost his job during the recession. Every day, he set out looking for work, but due to the

RISE AND THRIVE

economic crisis, companies were not hiring. He didn't want to sit at home doing nothing all day, so he decided to look for volunteer work. After several rejections, he was finally given an opportunity. The commitment and effort he put into his role, you would have thought he was being paid a large salary, but he was working for free. He arrived before anyone else, and was the last person to leave. The senior managers were so impressed with his work ethic that when one of the supervisors left, they immediately hired him and put him on the payroll. Don't underestimate the power of volunteering!

Trust Yourself: When you decide to start living your life's purpose, everyone is going to give you ten thousand reasons why you shouldn't be doing it. The way you choose to live your life has nothing to do with anyone but you, but people will still have something to say about it, especially if you do something risky, like quit your job to start a business. You will never hear the end of it. It's important to understand that when it comes to chasing your dreams, intuition overrides logic. Some of your friends and family members will be genuinely concerned about the new direction you are taking. They will worry about whether you will make enough money to survive. They will be afraid that you might lose some of the assets you've spent so many years accumulating. But you can't allow other people's fears to stop you from doing what you know is right. Depending on your intuition is the key to your success. Your purpose is what you were created to do here on Earth, and you will have a burning desire in your heart to do it. You won't know exactly how you are going to do it, but I can tell you from my personal experience that once you start doing it, everything will fall into place. You see, I believe in something called "divine timing," and it means that when you allow your heart to

113

guide you, you will be in the right place at the right time to receive the blessings the universe has for you.

Living a purpose-driven life requires planning. Once you've made up your mind about what you want to do, and you're working on overcoming your fears and stepping outside your comfort zone, the next step is to set goals and achieve them. In Chapter 5, you are going to learn exactly how to do that.

CHAPTER 5:

SEEING FROM WITHIN: SETTING AND ACHIEVING MEANINGFUL GOALS

The first two years of my self-development journey were spent doing things like visualizing, scripting, and trying to speak things into existence. After reading several books about the law of attraction, I became convinced that these were the things I needed to do to manifest my dream life. I kid you not; all the testimonies I read in these books gave the impression that all you needed to do was visualize, script, and speak, because everyone seemed to just magically fall into their dream lives after doing these things. As much as I believe in the law of attraction, one of the problems with its proponents is that they don't talk about the hard work that goes with applying the principles. Unless you have supernatural powers, no amount of thinking about something is going to make it tangible. The reason the law of attraction became so popular was because it offered an alternative to hard work—but the truth is that without hard work, the law of attraction does not work. Author Diana Rankin once said, "It takes twenty years of hard work to became an overnight success." While it may not take *everyone* twenty years to achieve their dreams, it does take a lot of hard work. When success-ful people appear to just pop out of nowhere, it's because they were doing the work for many years behind the scenes. Achieving your dreams is going to take hard work and determination, and the first step is to set goals the right way.

WHY PEOPLE DON'T ACHIEVE THEIR GOALS

A study conducted by the University of Scranton discovered that ninety-two percent of people who set goals fail to achieve them. I used to be a part of this statistic. Every year, for seven years, I would set three goals: to write my book; to lose weight; and to save money. None of them materialized until I started setting goals the right way. But there were also several other reasons why I wasn't achieving my goals. I later found out that my issues were a universal problem.

Success Is a Lifestyle: I've learned many lessons on my self-development journey, and one of them is that success should be a lifestyle and not something we attain every once in a while. I came to this conclusion after I finally managed to lose weight and then put it back on three months later. Why did I put it back on? Because healthy eating didn't become a lifestyle; it was something I did temporarily until I reached my ideal weight. Once I was happy with my body, I started making excuses to eat what I wanted again. I would say things like, "One donut won't hurt," but it was never one donut—I'd eat an entire tray of twelve! That binge would spark my sugar cravings, and before I knew it, I was right back to square one. Now, am I saying that you can't treat yourself every once in a while? No. But if you know that treating yourself leads to binge eating, treat yourself in a different way. I've learned how to make healthy versions of all the unhealthy foods I love. Eating these foods doesn't make me feel sluggish, and nor does it make me feel guilty.

Instead of focusing on making extreme improvements, aim to be one percent better at everything you do every day. In his book *Atomic Habits*, James Clear writes about the success of the British cycling team. The team had not won an Olympic gold medal in a hundred and ten years! In fact, they had become so famous for their terrible performances that a European bike manufacturer refused to sell their bikes to the team because they didn't want to destroy the name of their company. To improve the team's performance, the governing body for professional cycling in England hired a performance director called Dave Brailsford. The team had had several coaches over the century, but Brailsford implemented a strategy called "the aggregation of marginal gains." It involved making small improvements in everything the team did. Brailsford aimed to make a one-percent improvement in every area of bike riding. Over time, when put together, that one percent would make a significant improvement and transform the team into world-class athletes again.

Brailsford made tiny adjustments to everything including the bike seats, tires, clothing, massage gel, pillows, mattresses—he even had the riders try different hand-washing techniques! The team made hundreds of what appeared to be minor changes, but within five years, they won an astronomical sixty percent of the gold medals at the 2008 Beijing Olympics. Four years later, they broke seven world records at the Olympic Games in London. The wins continued for ten consecutive years; between 2007 to 2017, the team won a hundred and seventy-eight world championships and sixty-six Olympic gold medals!

While the team were making these small changes, I am sure they were getting frustrated with it because at first it would have seemed pointless. But as they learned, within five years, those minor changes led to a culture of winning. When I adopted this method with weight loss and healthy eating, it seemed pointless at first, but within a year, my entire life had changed and I haven't looked back since. After taking the extreme route, experiencing multiple failures and getting terribly frustrated because I started believing I was incapable of changing my life, I read *Atomic Habits*, tried the one percent rule—and it worked. Making small changes works because when we make extreme changes, it becomes mentally and physically exhausting and it's not sustainable. I got the fast results I wanted by eating only vegetables and salads for three months, but it wasn't sustainable—hence I put the weight back on just as quickly as I had lost it.

Making success a lifestyle doesn't just apply to weight loss; it applies to every area of your life. If you want to save more money, read more, improve your relationships, or become more organized, make small changes every day, and you'll be amazed at what you achieve within one year. I challenge you to do this with a maximum of three things so you don't overwhelm yourself—and watch what happens in twelve months.

Failure to Plan: Benjamin Franklin once said, "If you fail to plan, you are planning to fail." In other words, if you don't plan your success, you're just stumbling around in the dark hoping for the best. Winging it has never got anyone anywhere. There is not one single successful person in the world who just fell into success—it was planned and it was strategic. And if you don't have a plan, like Benjamin Franklin rightly put it, you can expect to fail.

Planning provides a roadmap to success; it guides and directs us so that even if we end up going in the wrong direction, our plan will always get us back on track. It's important to mention here that you can be the most meticulous planner, but you will always run into obstacles because that's life. But once you understand this, you won't find it so stressful to reevaluate your plan and make the necessary adjustments. Additionally, planning enables you to anticipate obstacles so you can plan ahead.

Planning gives you direction and clarity. It allows you to take the small, manageable steps you need in order to achieve your main goal. Goal-setting is easy, and making a plan feels great, but the size of the goal might scare you and cause you to shrink back from it. Planning helps you track your progress so you can stay motivated, and motivation is essential when it comes to achieving your goals.

Finally, achieving your goals requires a variety of resources. Planning helps you identify those resources, determine how you will acquire them, and how you will manage them. Without a plan, resources go to waste and this can cause you to get into debt, which forces you to abandon your dreams. You might have plenty of drive, but when the resources run dry, no amount of drive will get you back on track. I'm not saying that finances won't dwindle while you are working on your goals, because for some of you, it's going to be about trial and error—you won't know what will and won't work until you try. However, a solid plan will ensure your waste is minimal.

Procrastination: We have all heard the saying, "Procrastination is the thief of time," and we all know how true it is. How many times have you promised yourself that you would start working on your goals only to end up doing everything but work on your goals? This doesn't just happen once or twice, but day after day, month after month, and year after year. Procrastination will most definitely steal your time. You will then find yourself making all sorts of excuses to yourself, friends, and family members about why you haven't achieved what you set out to achieve. But the reality is that there is no one and nothing in this world to blame but yourself. Playing the blame game feels good temporarily because no one knows what you are doing behind closed doors. While you are telling everyone that the kids are too much of a distraction, or it's because of your chronic sickness, no one sees you hit the snooze button until you've got minutes to spare before you're late for work. Nor do they see you scrolling for hours at a time until you pass out in front of the TV. To the average person, your excuses are understandable. But when you lay your head down to sleep at night, you know in your heart that you are wasting time, and that if you had a bit more self-discipline, you could get so much more done. Don't allow procrastination to rob you of the life you want to live.

We Don't Write Them Down: Another interesting statistic is that you are forty-two percent more likely to achieve your goals if you write them down. This one simple act changes vague intentions into clear objectives that you can actually read instead of think about. For several years, my New Year's resolutions stayed in my head. I mentioned them to loved ones, but that was as far as it went. In January, I was all motivated, but by February, the excuses started rolling in. It wasn't long before I stopped mentioning them altogether. Within a few months, I'd promise myself I would start again the following year. But every year, the cycle would repeat itself.

Writing down your goals is essential for success. First of all, it provides focus and clarity; they are no longer ideas floating around in your head that either remain ambiguous, or you eventually forget. Writing them down forces you to articulate exactly what you want to achieve. It helps you to prioritize, organize, and evaluate them. Most people don't have just one goal; they have several. Mine were always to write a book, save more money, and lose weight. Looking at them at face value, it appears there are only three goals.

But once I began breaking them down, this number more than doubled. What happens when you write your goals down is that you start asking yourself questions and answering them. I wanted to save more money to travel the world, buy a house, get married, save for my children's college funds, and the list went on. Once I had this information, I couldn't ignore it, I couldn't shrink my goals; these were all things I wanted out of life. Anyway, more on writing your goals down later, but what I can say for now is that it worked! Things started changing for me once I became crystal clear about what I wanted to achieve, and this clarity only came once I had written my goals down.

We Get Discouraged: As a child, I really loved my grandma's Sunday roast dinner. My mom, dad, sisters and I would turn up at her house, and I could smell the delicious aromas of gravy, meat, and potatoes as soon as I stepped out of the car. We would go into the house, and my grandma would have laid all the food out on the table and we'd sit down to eat. It wasn't until I was a teenager and I would sometimes stay with my grandma over the weekend that I learned why her Sunday roasts tasted so good. She spent twenty-four hours cooking it! At thirteen years old, I didn't understand how the principle of slow cooking applied to goal achievement, but now I do.

We live in a "now culture," and it is consistently reinforced by society. If you want the body of your dreams, get plastic surgery. If you want to get rich, play the lottery. If you want something you can't afford, get into debt and buy it on finance. Discipline, patience, and hard work are foreign concepts to the average person today, which is one of the reasons your friends and family will change their behavior towards you when you start working on your goals (more on that in Chapter 7). My granny's Sunday roast was so delicious because she spent so much time preparing it. The more time you invest in your goals, the better the end results will be. But the problem is that we get discouraged when we don't see immediate results, and we give up.

I remember trying to lose weight each year. I knew what I wanted to look like, but the difference between how I looked at the time and my end goal was so significant that I would lose motivation. I went to the gym, and changed my diet, but because I couldn't see my abs within a month, I would throw in the towel and opt for the immediate gratification of stuffing my face with cream donuts. Dreaming about what I wanted to look like felt good, but doing the work to achieve it didn't. I comforted myself by eating unhealthy food, and I got trapped in a vicious cycle that caused me to put on more weight.

While I love how technology makes my life so much easier, it has greatly enforced the culture of instant gratification. Today, people have become accustomed to getting what they want when they want it, which makes it so much easier to fail. Take my weight loss journey, for example. I would empty my cupboards, get rid of all my unhealthy snacks, and refill them with healthy food. But when the craving hit, or I got discouraged, I didn't even need to take a trip to the store—I'd order what I wanted online, and it would be at my door within thirty minutes. This expectation of getting what you want when you want it creeps into other areas of life, such as personal and professional goals. When we don't see immediate results, we get frustrated, which makes us doubt ourselves and start thinking about whether it's even possible to achieve the goals we've set.

It's human nature to seek pleasure and not pain. Our brains are wired that way. Psychologists refer to this as the "pleasure principle." Achieving long-term goals requires making short-term sacrifices without any rewards. This creates a mental conflict that makes it difficult to stay motivated. With me, I would think to myself, "What's the point in doing this? It's been a month of no fast food, sweating like a pig at the gym, and my stomach is still hanging over my trousers." By consistently thinking like this, I convinced myself to give up. With each failure, I felt increasingly inadequate and I believed in myself less and less. When you don't believe in yourself, it is very easy to become a quitter.

Social media was another instrument of discouragement that made me feel even more unworthy. I watched a lot of success stories about people who had achieved massive success, whether it was establishing a business, losing weight, or finding their ideal partner. All these highlights skewed my perception of reality because all I was seeing was end results, so it made it seem as if their success was effortless. I got stuck in a comparison trap where I overlooked the hard work these people put in to achieving their goals.

S.M.A.R.T Goals – How to Set Goals the Right Way

I had always heard people talk about "vision" but I didn't quite understand it because as far as I was concerned, vision related to eyesight—you know, when you visit the optician's and they check your eyesight and give you a score, with the highest being twenty-twenty vision. To me, vision was about what you could see with your natural eyes. But one day, when I was writing my book, it dawned on me that vision has nothing to do with what you can see with your physical eyes—it's about what you can see with your spiritual eyes. Your spirit lives within you; it's the part of you that you can't see, and it has eyes. I am not saying this is a scientific fact, but there is definitely something to it. Some people refer to it as our "imagination," which also makes sense. But however you want to look at it, human beings see the invisible before they see the visible. Sounds crazy, right? But let me explain. I will use Jeff Bezos and Amazon as an example.

Okay, for those of you who don't know, Jeff Bezos is the founder of the online store Amazon we have all grown to love and depend on significantly (I know I have). But before it came to fruition, Bezos had a vision of building an online store where customers could buy anything and everything. Now, this was in 1994 when the power of the Internet had not yet been actualized—but he saw ahead, not with his physical eyes, but with his spiritual eyes. And there were very few people who could see what he saw, because when he attempted to raise one million dollars to get started, he only managed to convince twenty-two out of the sixty people he approached to make an investment. To the majority of people, what Bezos wanted to achieve sounded ridiculous. I am sure those thirty-eight individuals who rejected him are kicking themselves now! Nevertheless, everything Jeff Bezos saw with his spiritual eyes, he can now see with his physical eyes—and so can the rest of the world.

I said all that to say this: This section is about getting what you can see with your spiritual eyes down on paper. This is the first step in turning your dreams into reality. As you've read, ninety-two percent of people never achieve their goals, and one of the reasons for this is that they don't write them down. But it is not just about writing them down—there's a strategy to it. In this chapter, I'm going to teach you exactly how to use it.

S.M.A.R.T is the acronym for Specific, Measurable, Achievable, Relevant, and Time-bound. Without implementing this strategy, you'll feel as if you're running on the treadmill of life and not getting anywhere. You might want to become a business owner in the next five years, but in your current position, it seems absolutely impossible. I can tell you with confidence that it's not—if you're willing to do the work. I'll give you some additional tips on goal attainment shortly, but to start, here is a breakdown of the S.M.A.R.T method:

Specific: What exactly do you want to achieve? To get a clear picture of your goal, ask yourself the following questions:

- What do I want to achieve?
- Why do I want to achieve this goal?
- Is anyone going to help me to achieve this goal?
- Does this goal involve a location?
- What resources will I need to achieve this goal?
- Are there any limitations to this goal?

Measurable: Making progress is essential to goal achievement because it motivates you to continue. When you have a large goal, focusing on the destination gets overwhelming because it can seem as if you will never get there. For example, let's say you want to lose a hundred pounds. While many people have achieved this feat, it's a lot of weight to lose. Instead of just saying that you aim to lose a hundred pounds, aim to lose two pounds per week. This way, you can track your progress. Have a sheet up in front of your weighing scale and cross off the pounds as you go. Two pounds per week doesn't seem like a lot of weight and you won't notice the different right away. But as the scales keep reminding you that you're winning, you will feel motivated to continue. Within a few months, people will start congratulating you on your weight loss. That's when you'll truly start noticing that your efforts are paying off.

Achievable: I am a believer in having big dreams. I also believe you can achieve anything you put your mind to if you are serious about achieving it. However, being realistic about your goals is important or you will get discouraged and give up. I did this every year until I changed my approach to goal achievement. One year I said I would write my book within three months! Those three months came and went, and I hadn't even written ten pages. Don't set yourself up for failure by giving yourself unreasonable timeframes to achieve your goals, or you will keep getting disappointed. The more you fail, the less confidence you will have in yourself, and you need confidence if you are going to win at this game.

Relevant: There are some people who will set goals just because their friends are setting them. Or because they are in competition with someone. Don't waste time setting goals that are not relevant to what you want to achieve in life. Whatever goals you set for yourself, think about the *why* behind it. If you have an ulterior motive other than to improve your life, don't bother.

Time-bound: Business man Robert Herjavec once said, "A goal without a deadline is just a dream." What he meant is that if you don't put a date on your goal, there won't be any urgency attached to it and you will most likely never get around to working on it. Research suggests that this is true. According to Parkinson's law, not having a deadline backfires. The law came about after a group of researchers studied people who worked to a tight deadline, and those who had extra time to complete their work. They found that those with a tight deadline worked hard to complete the task, but the participants who had extra time waited until the last minute to complete the task. Basically, when we have too much time on our hands, we procrastinate. However, when you give yourself a date by which to achieve a goal, you can measure your progress, which means you are more likely to achieve it. Let's go back to the weight loss goal. To lose a hundred pounds in one year, you aim to lose two pounds per week. If half way through the year, you notice that your weight loss has plateaued, you might need to alter your routine to see if anything changes. This could take a while, so once the weight starts shifting again, give yourself a new deadline. If you end up missing your deadline, don't beat yourself up about it—just set yourself a new one and keep going.

ADDITIONAL TIPS FOR GOAL ATTAINMENT

Planning is the easiest part of goal achievement; once you've got everything written down, it all looks wonderful. But then comes the dreaded task of doing the work—and this is where a lot of people hit a brick wall because even though they now have a roadmap, organizing your life to actually get stuff done is challenging. This is especially true if you've got children, a partner, or you live with people who are not on the same page as you. Nevertheless, here are a few tips that helped me achieve my goals—I still use them to this day.

Get Organized: Do you live in a messy environment like I did? Research suggests that clutter has a negative effect on our performance. According to a study published in the National Library of Medicine, our brains are wired for order, and a messy environment drains our mental resources, making it difficult to focus. Physical clutter can cause stress and anxiety because you are subconsciously thinking about the mess you need to clean up.

Before you start working on your goals, tidy your house. If you occupy one room, give it a good clean, get rid of any clutter, and create a space with a desk and a chair so you can work. Do the same if you live in a house—create an office space free from distractions.

A Daily Routine: Lao Tzu once said, "A journey of a thousand miles begins with one step." A daily routine helps you put one foot in front of the other and build the habits required to achieve your goals. Everyone has a daily routine, but nine times out of ten it's not productive. I used to wake up minutes before I was due to start work, rush around getting dressed, jump in the car, head to the Mc-Donald's drive-through, and eat breakfast one-handed while driving to work. That was my life for many years. I engaged in terrible habits that kept me in a perpetual cycle of failure. But once I got into a productive daily routine, things changed.

The first goal I set for myself was to lose weight. So, I started waking up one hour early to cycle. It's important to mention here that when it comes to a daily routine, do the thing that's easiest for you, in order to succeed. Initially, I joined a gym and tried waking up two hours early to get there. I probably went to the gym twice in the first month when my aim was to go three times per week. I quickly realized that going to the gym first thing in the morning wasn't a good idea, so I promised myself I would go after work. That didn't work either because I always made the excuse that I was too tired. After explaining my struggles to my mentor, she suggested that I work out from home, as my subconscious mind was struggling to get used to my new routine because it was such a large mental shift. I had gone from rolling out of bed a few minutes before work to waking up two hours earlier than my body was used to. Jackie advised me to go to bed thirty minutes earlier than usual and wake up thirty minutes earlier so I wouldn't feel so drained. I then did a ten-minute cycle routine. Ten minutes isn't a lot of time when the Centers for Disease Control advises adults to spend thirty minutes a day doing moderate-intensity physical activity. However, when you are some-one who hasn't worked out a day in your life, starting at ten minutes a day is better than nothing. I did this for ninety days straight. After this, exercise had developed into a habit and I increased the time. Today, I exercise for no less than one hour per day.

Whatever you want to achieve, incorporate it into your daily routine, even if it's just for ten minutes a day. Again, the key is to start small or you will overwhelm yourself and give up before you've even started. Those small steps you take will add up, and it will inspire you to keep working on your goals.

Vision Board: While it's impossible to work on all of your goals at once, it is possible to remind yourself of them daily. A vision board will help you do this. It's a simple exercise that allows you to transform your goals into a collage so you can see them every day. When you keep your goals at the forefront of your mind, you are more likely to achieve them. Here's how to create your very own vision board:

- Buy a large board (the size is up to you; just make sure you've got the space to hang it up).

- Find images of your vision online or in magazines/newspapers and cut them out.

- Find words that describe your vision online or in magazines/newspapers and cut them out.

- Stick your images and words on your vision board. Make it look as pretty as you want.

- Hang your vision board somewhere you will see it every day.

- Every day, stand in front of your vision board and take it all in. Imagine yourself achieving each and every goal you have set for yourself.

I make a new vision board every year, because now I know how to set and achieve goals, I fly through them. Over the past five years, not a year has gone by that I haven't achieved each and every goal that I've set for myself, and I am so proud to be able to say this. I want you to be able to say the same because it's such an awesome feeling.

Break It Down: I struggled with all of my goals, but the one I struggled with the most was weight loss and living a healthy lifestyle. In my mind, doing without all those delicious foods was impossible. But when I learned that what I was experiencing was more than a lack of self-discipline—I was actually addicted to junk food—it became easier to kick the habit. Like any addiction, whether it's drugs, alcohol, or cigarettes, the key is to wean you off it. Smokers use Nicorette patches because they are still getting some nicotine, and therefore the craving is relieved. Month by month, or week by week, smokers decrease the strength of the nicotine patch until they no longer need it. I used the same approach with food. I kicked the habit one soda, one chocolate bar, and one burger at a time. Some people manage to beat their addiction by going cold turkey, but that wasn't my story. I tried several times, but it wasn't working, so I had to try something else. You know what they say: "Insanity is doing the same thing over and over again and expecting different results." By slowly weaning myself off junk food, I eventually kicked the habit for good. I did it month by month. I started by replacing my sodas with water, but I still ate junk food for breakfast, lunch, and dinner. Once I'd kicked the soda habit, I replaced breakfast with something healthy; I'd eat the same food, but make a healthier version of it. I continued this until I was finally eating a healthy meal for breakfast, lunch, and dinner. As I write this section, I can't tell you the last time I ate junk food!

Small Daily Habits: As mentioned, success should be a lifestyle and not something you achieve every once in a while. That's why now, I write something every day. Even if I'm not writing a book, for me, it's about skill development. Improving my writing skills is something I can do continuously. Becoming the best version of yourself should be something you aspire to until the day you die, because there will always be room for improvement.

Whatever you want to achieve, turn it into a small daily habit. Another reason people don't achieve their goals is because they become overwhelmed with the magnitude of them. But by working on your goal one day at a time, you will eventually achieve it. Additionally, this approach forces you to focus on your goal every day, even if it's just for five minutes at time. Remember the one percent improvement theory? The little bit you do each day will eventually lead to you completing that goal. Once you've completed it, celebrate your success, and move on to the next.

Accountability Partner: An accountability partner is either a successful person who has already achieved a lot in life, or someone who is just as determined as you to achieve your goals. Remember, the blind can't lead the blind or you will both end up in a pit together. This was one of the many lessons I learned on my self-development journey. As mentioned, my friends and I were always really enthusiastic about achieving our goals in January, but by the end of February, we had all fallen off. I convinced one of my friends to do the S.M.A.R.T method, which she did, and then we decided to become accountability partners. Neither of us were strong enough to resist the temptation to indulge in the habits that pulled us away from working on our goals, and it wasn't long before we both decided to call it quits and try again next year. But when I met my mentor Jackie, she was having none of it. In fact, I was scared to tell her that I hadn't completed my chapter because I'd decided to binge-watch my favorite series on Netflix. Jackie pushed me to my limit. She brought out all the excellence that was lying dormant within me. I grew in ways I didn't think were possible. I became the woman I saw in my head—and I am proud of myself. Find an accountability partner who won't tolerate you slacking off, and you will be amazed at what you can achieve.

Writing down your goals is essential for anyone who is serious about achieving them. Without a clear idea about what you want to achieve, you'll just keep shooting in the dark hoping to hit something. The more you miss the mark, the more discouraged you will become, and eventually, you will give up. But by applying the strategies set out in this chapter, you can expect to achieve your dreams one goal at a time.

Women are renowned for putting everyone first, before themselves—whether it's their children, their partner, friends, or family members. While giving of yourself is very rewarding, it's also draining. As the saying goes, "You can't pour from an empty cup," and this is what happens to a lot of female empaths and highly sensitive people; they keep giving and giving until they've got nothing left to give and end up completely exhausted. But from today, I want you to become selfish and proud of it, because if you are going to live the life you know you truly deserve, you need to put yourself first. In Chapter 6, I'm going to show you exactly how to do this.

CHAPTER 6:

SELFISH AND PROUD: HOW TO PUT YOURSELF FIRST IN EVERY SITUATION

used to get extremely offended when anyone called me selfish, and then feel guilty that I wasn't putting someone else's needs before my own. But once I started developing inner strength, I realized that the people who called me selfish were toxic and they used the term to manipulate me into doing what they wanted me to do. As soon as I was shamed for feeling bad about saying no to a request, I would end up doing it because I didn't like confrontation and I didn't want to upset anyone. But it made me resentful because most of the time, what this friend, family member, or co-worker wanted me to do was an inconvenience. I was always frustrated and stressed out because I was constantly carrying loads that were too heavy for me. But once I set myself free from the chains of people-pleasing, my life changed for the better. If anyone were to dare call me selfish today, I would take it as a compliment and thank them. If you are going to become the woman you know are destined to be, selfishness is a must. Here is some insight into the power of selfishness and how it can transform your life:

THE SELFISHNESS DILEMMA

I believe that every single human being on the planet is selfish because if you don't think about yourself first, you won't survive. Not only is selfishness about survival—if you don't take care of yourself, you won't be able to take care of anyone else. When you are traveling on an airplane, before the flight takes off, the flight attendant will advise all passengers of what to do in an emergency, and the first instruction is to put their oxygen masks on before they help anyone else, even their own children. This is because if they run out of oxygen, they won't be much use to anyone struggling with their oxygen mask. The same rule applies in life: Take care of yourself first so you will have the mental and physical capacity to take care of others. However, the word "selfish" is typically used as an insult to describe someone who doesn't care about anyone but themselves. They are ruthless, cutthroat individuals who will step on anyone to get ahead. That's not the type of selfish we will be focusing on in this chapter. This definition of "selfish" is why people get offended when someone refers to them as such. But rarely do we hear about the second definition of "selfish," which refers to a person understanding their needs, prioritizing them, and articulating them when necessary.

There is value in selfishness, and this has been grossly misunderstood to the point where we do things that we don't want to do to avoid being thought of as selfish. This happens in romantic relationships, platonic relationships, families, and work relationships. The result? We get frustrated, resent our loved ones, and end up completely burned out from always taking on more than we can handle. When it comes to selfishness, it's about balance.

WHAT HEALTHY SELFISHNESS LOOKS LIKE

According to humanistic psychologist Scott Barry Kaufman, healthy selfishness is having the courage to say no without causing offense—but not feeling bad if you do cause offense. This used to be my dilemma. I had all the courage in the world to say no when someone asked me to do something I either didn't want to do or didn't have the capacity to do. But when they got offended, or made me feel guilty, I would fold. In Kaufman's research, he found that people who practiced healthy selfishness were more content with life, more self-compassionate, less depressed, and had a positive outlook in general. When they did help others, it wasn't because they wanted something in return, a pat on the back, or social recognition. They did it out of the goodness of their heart. The Dalai Lama refers to this as *wise selfishness*, where you take pride in serving others because it benefits you more than anyone else. Plenty of studies prove that those with a giving nature are happier. But you are not so giving that your own needs go unmet. The lines between healthy and unhealthy selfishness are so blurred that most people are not sure how to practice healthy selfishness. If you want more time to yourself so you can work on your goals and improve your life, keep reading.

EXAMPLES OF HEALTHY SELFISHNESS

Until I started reading about healthy selfishness, I had no idea what it was; therefore, I am assuming some of you reading this are in the same boat. Here are some examples of what healthy selfishness looks like:

Saying No: When someone asks you to do something you either can't fit into your schedule, or you have no interest in doing, just say no. It's okay to make small sacrifices every once in a while, but if you can't do it, just say no, even if the person asking gets offended.

Pursuing Your Goals: You will be shocked at how the people closest to you will change their behavior towards you once you start pursuing your goals. There are many reasons for this, but one of them is that working on your goals requires you to make sacrifices, which means you won't be able to hang out as much. As a result, the dynamics of your relationships will shift (more on this in Chapter 7), and they won't like it. At this point, you will need to make a choice and decide what's more important to you—maintaining your relationships or achieving your goals.

Alone Time: Empaths and highly sensitive people value alone time more than the average person because that's how they rejuvenate their minds, refresh their souls, and reconnect with themselves. How you spend your alone time is up to you, but it could mean going for a walk, reading a book, or doing something creative like drawing or sculpting.

Prioritizing Your Health: Your physical, mental, spiritual, and emotional health is essential to your overall well-being, and therefore prioritizing it is a must. This means if you feel ill, visit the doctor as soon as possible. If your mental health is suffering, speak to someone you trust or find a good therapist if you don't already have one. Additionally, don't wait until an area of your health is suffering to nurture it—nurture your health daily.

Setting Boundaries: Boundaries are the invisible lines we place around ourselves that let people know how far they can go. Establishing healthy boundaries with your loved ones and co-workers protects your mental health, prevents you from being taken advantage of, and shields you from having to deal with behavior that makes you uncomfortable.

Doing What You Love: Doing the things you love is a great way to practice healthy selfishness because they are your hobbies and interests that make you content and happy. When you are content and happy, it is easier to pour into the lives of others.

How to Practice Healthy Selfishness

When I first started practicing healthy selfishness, I found it difficult because I was so used to fulfilling everyone else's needs that I didn't even know what mine were. It took a while to remember to think of myself first. But once I experienced the benefits of healthy self-ishness, I didn't look back. Here are some tips on how to practice healthy selfishness:

Learn to Say No: Learning how to say no can be difficult for most people, but even more so for highly sensitive people and empaths because you are usually the one whom everyone goes to when they need help. But what people don't realize is that, although you don't mind helping out, you often take on more than you can handle because you don't want to cause offense. As a result, you end up burned out and exhausted. You can avoid this by learning to say no when you don't have the mental or physical capacity to help. Here are some tips on how to say no:

- **No Explanation:** You have every right to say no to a re-quest if you don't want to do it, and you have every right not to give an explanation. When I started practicing this, it was a game changer. If I ever said no to something, I gave the person a long-winded explanation as to why I wasn't able to do it because I thought that was the polite thing to do. But what I found was that giving explanations gives the person the opportunity to pull you in. For example, you might say, "I'm really sorry but I can't help you re-write your résumé today because I'm having lunch with a friend." They will reply, "Oh, that's fine. We can work on it when you get back. Just give me a call when you're ready." Unless you are a quick thinker, it will be hard to get out of this. However, when you just say no without providing an explanation, the person is less likely to ask for a reason because deep down, they know it's none of their business.

- **Be Assertive:** Assertiveness will protect you from pushy people. By choosing firm and definitive words, you take the power out of the person's hands so they can't negotiate with you. They will know you mean business and back off. This is a great approach to use at work with managers and co-workers who feel it's their life's purpose to dump piles of work on you. The next time someone tries to burden you with extra tasks, say something like, "I'm sorry, but helping you at the moment is impossible—I'm working on several deadlines and I don't have the time to spare."

- **Stand Your Ground:** As mentioned, after giving an explanation as to why you can't do something, some people won't take no for an answer and will keep pushing the issue. Stand your ground and don't allow anyone to convince you to do something you don't want to do. You are not being selfish (in the negative sense); you are simply putting your needs first and there is nothing wrong with that. Let the person think what they want to think—it's not your problem.

- **Check Your Schedule:** I found that one of the most effective ways for me to say no is to respond with something like, "I'm not sure, but let me check my schedule and I'll get back to you." I did this during face-to-face interactions when I didn't feel comfortable saying no. I would call the person later and explain that I had a full schedule and I wasn't able to help out. I found it so much easier to reject people over the phone as they couldn't see my facial expressions and I usually look nervous when I'm not comfortable with something. When people detect a lack of confidence, they take advantage of you.

Set Boundaries: Setting boundaries is another difficult necessity in life, and you will probably feel guilty when you start because it's new to your loved ones and they might feel as if you are rejecting them. But for the sake of your mental health and to give yourself the time you need to invest in self-care so you have what you need to give to others, establishing clear boundaries in your life is essential. You should set boundaries in your romantic and platonic relationships, at home, and at work. You can apply the following suggestions across the board.

- **Reflect:** To establish healthy boundaries, you need to know what boundaries to erect. Start by reflecting on your relationships to determine what changes you need to make. Get yourself a journal and write everything down. Here are some questions to consider:
  - How do people invade my space?
  - When do I feel the most disrespected and uncomfortable?

- How do I feel when I know my boundaries have been crossed?
- What are the physical, mental, and emotional limits I need to establish to protect my well-being?
- How can I articulate my boundaries to people in a way that they will understand and doesn't cause offense?
- What consequences will I enforce if my boundaries are not taken seriously?
- What boundaries will I establish in my professional and private life?
- How can I prioritize my needs when I am establishing my boundaries?
- How do I manage feelings of discomfort and guilt when I am establishing boundaries?
- What resources or support do I need to help me establish boundaries?

Once you have a clear understanding of the boundaries you wish to establish, don't back down from them. As mentioned, it will be hard because this isn't something you have done before, and your loved ones won't like it. However, this isn't about them—it's about you, so stick to the plan.

- **Enforce:** Now that you've decided to set boundaries, you don't need to call everyone in your life and tell them so. Start the conversation when your boundaries are violated. For example, your manager always storms into your office and slams a pile of papers down on your desk demanding that the work is done by a certain time. But the work is never your work—it's his. And he never asks if you can fit it in—he just expects you to do it. Ask him to come into your office, shut the door and have a seat. Then politely inform your manager that you can't help out because you are working on your own projects, and in future, if he needs your assistance, can he ask instead of demanding. To protect yourself further, remind him of what is written in your job description and that you are not paid overtime to do his work. If your manager chooses to ignore your boundaries or attempts to use his authority to scare you into doing the work, let him know you will be reporting him to the human resources department. Reporting is the consequence for violating your boundaries.

- **Consequences:** Some people are going to violate your boundaries intentionally. These are the individuals who are so used to having complete access to your life and you never saying no to them that your boundaries are offensive. Therefore, they will violate your boundaries to test whether you are serious. I operate on a "three strikes and you're out" policy; it usually works, but sometimes it doesn't. I opted for the "three strikes" policy because it's easy for people to forget when this is the first time they've heard your boundaries communicated, so you will need to give them some grace. If this individual continues violating your boundaries after the third strike, enforce the consequences with no remorse. If they continue violating your boundaries after you've enforced the consequences, end the relationship. I have also had to do this. Someone who continuously violates your boundaries has no respect for you and doesn't deserve space in your life.

Prioritize Self-Care: In today's society, where busyness has become the norm, burnout has also become the norm. Women run themselves into the ground working, raising children, and maintaining relationships. For most of us, doing the basics is difficult enough, let alone setting aside time for self-care. But self-care isn't something we should do every once in a while—it should be a part of our daily routine. "Daily routine! I don't even have time to use the bathroom in peace without my little one banging on the door for me to get out." I felt the same way when I first read about the importance of self-care; I truly believed I didn't have the time for it. But once I evaluated my life, I realized I had plenty of time, and I'm sure you do too. You see, we are really good at doing two things: wasting time, and giving the appearance of busyness. Research suggests that globally, we spend an average of six hours and forty minutes per day in front of a screen. What's even worse is that this screen time is spent on unproductive activities such as scrolling through social media and playing games. When I took an inventory of my life to determine where I was wasting the most time, I wasn't surprised to find that it was on my phone. I checked it as soon as I woke up in the morning, on every break at work, after work, when I sat in my car, when I ate dinner, after dinner, and before I went to bed. I had to accept the fact that I was addicted to my phone and that I was allowing it to steal my time.

I started off by replacing five minutes per day of screen time with meditation. Oh, my goodness! It was the best decision I ever made because I felt awesome, and it encouraged me to keep working on myself. As soon as I came out of the meditation and my mind was refreshed and clear, I wanted to remain in that state, and so, instead of picking up my phone, I would read a book or do something else that would benefit me. It took me just over a year to beat my phone and scrolling addiction. Today I spend half an hour a day on the phone and that's doing productive things like replying to messages or reaching out to loved ones. I do all my binge-watching on Sundays. I still watch my favorite shows on Netflix, and I still check out social media—I just don't do it excessively. I can confidently say that my phone no longer consumes my days. To start prioritizing self-care, do the following:

- **Evaluate Your Life:** Most women say they would love to prioritize self-care but they don't have the time. I can guarantee you have more than one hour per day to spend on self-care. Once you take inventory of your life, you will discover that you waste a lot of time on fruitless activities. To take inventory of your life, spend your busiest day recording everything you do, from the moment you wake up to the moment you go to bed. Pay attention to the following:

  – How many times do you hit the snooze button?

  – What do you do on your phone?

  – How long do you spend watching TV?

  – What do you do when you are driving?

  – How many times are you interrupted by friends, family members, and co-workers?

  – Do you procrastinate?

  – Do you multitask?

  – How much time do you spend checking your emails?

  – What random activities or errands distract you from your planned schedule?

  – How many meetings do you have? Are they effective?

  – How many breaks do you take throughout the day?

- How many times do you stop what you are doing for a snack?

- How much time do you spend preparing and planning?

- How long do you spend talking on the phone?

Once you have taken inventory of your life, determine the areas where you are wasting time and use that time for self-care activities.

- **Identify Your Needs:** Our self-care needs are different; what works for one woman might not work for you. Therefore, determine your personal self-care needs and apply them to your life. Here are some tips to help you identify your self-care needs:

  - **Stress:** Stress reduction is an important part of self-care. While a certain level of stress is normal, some people, environments, or situations contribute to an unhealthy level of stress. Determine what these things are and eliminate them.

  - **Priorities:** What are your goals and values? What are the things that are most important in your life? Prioritizing them is a form of self-care.

  - **Physical Signs:** Listen to your body. It will let you know when you need some tender loving care. Symptoms such as muscle tension, headaches, and excessive tiredness are all signs that you need to take better care of yourself.

  - **Emotions:** Pay attention to your moods and your emotional response to situations and people. Are there any patterns that trigger negative emotions?

- **Energy Levels:** When do you feel the most energetic, and when do you feel the most drained? Identify these interactions and make the necessary changes.

• **Schedule It:** Self-care has been scientifically proven to reduce stress, anxiety, and depression. Self-care makes you less angry and frustrated, improves energy levels, and makes you happier. These are just a few of the benefits of practicing self-care. However, to experience the fullness of these benefits, self-care should be something you practice daily. Schedule time during your day for self-care. It could be in the morning, afternoon, or in the evening. Choose a time that's most convenient for you and stick to it.

• **Self-Care Ideas:** You may already have some ideas about which self-care practices to engage in, but if you're not sure, here are a few to get you started:

  - **Meditation:** Meditation has many benefits including stress reduction, improved mental clarity, and encouraging mindfulness. Like me, you will notice the benefits by practicing meditation for five minutes per day. A great way to get started is with guided meditation—a quick Google search will help you find one.

  - **Exercise:** Moving your body is an essential part of self-care because it strengthens the heart, helps with weight management, and boosts mental health and emotional well-being. There are many ways to exercise including jogging, skipping, playing sports, or going to the gym.

  - **Read:** Reading is an enriching form of self-care and provides many benefits including relaxation, mental escape, and improved memory and concentration.

- **Journal:** Journaling is a powerful form of self-expression. It provides you with a safe space to release your emotions without the fear of being judged. Research suggests that journaling improves your self-awareness, reduces stress and anxiety, and encourages personal growth.

- **Creative Hobbies:** Doing the things you love makes you feel good. When you immerse yourself in your hobbies, your brain releases chemicals such as dopamine, which contribute to your happiness.

- **Nature Walks:** Get out in nature and walk amongst the plants, trees and flowers. By exposing yourself to the sunlight and breathing in fresh air, you improve your mental, emotional, and physical well-being.

- **Spa Day:** If you enjoy going to the spa but it's not something you can afford to do often, create your own spa day at home. Create a calm and soothing atmosphere with scented candles. Use essential oils like chamomile, eucalyptus, or lavender in a diffuser. Play relaxing music, and then start working on your skincare, hair, and body. Give yourself a manicure and pedicure, massage your scalp, exfoliate your body and take a long, relaxing bath.

• **Experiment:** As you've just read, there are plenty of ways to practice self-care, but it's about what works best for you. Experiment with different self-care practices to determine what to stick to.

Protect Your Energy: Empaths and highly sensitive people have a very good understanding of energy because they are always tuned into it. You can walk into a room and feel whether the atmosphere is good or bad. You can sense when someone is staring at you when your back is turned, or your instincts will alert you when you are dealing with a person carrying negative energy. Because of your strong connection to energy, it is easy for you to become consumed by it and end up feeling overwhelmed and burned out. Protecting your energy is essential for practicing healthy selfishness. Here are a few reasons why:

- Your day starts off great, you are excited about life—but then, whether it comes from social media, a person, or a situation, you expose yourself to something negative. You completely absorb the negative emotion, and you can't shake it off for the rest of the day.

- You've received some good news, and you can't wait to meet up with a friend and share it with her. But as soon as you sit down, she's complaining about something. You join her in her complaint, and now your good news doesn't matter anymore.

- You haven't had the best day at work, you get home, and your partner is equally as stressed out. It's not long before you are having a massive argument about nothing.

In each of these situations, you can see how easy it is to absorb someone else's energy without even thinking about it. Not only do you absorb the energy, it influences you to act in a certain way, and when the energy is negative, so is your behavior.

Protecting your energy isn't about avoiding negative emotions, because negative emotions are a part of the human experience. However, it's not your responsibility to process other people's emotions, no matter who they belong to. Having the ability to tune into the energy of others is a powerful gift—but it can work against you if you don't know how to protect your energy. The question is, how do you protect your energy? There are many ways to achieve this. Here are some of them:

- **Shield Yourself:** As awesome as it would be to live in a world with no negative energy, that's not going to happen. The only thing we can do is protect ourselves against it. It's unrealistic to expect everyone to be positive all the time—that's another thing that will never happen—but what we can do is shield ourselves against the negative energy flowing from other people. Shielding was another game changer for me because I became very intentional about what I allowed into my space. When you've done the work to protect yourself against negative energy, you are going to pay more attention to your surroundings. I used to walk into negative environments or situations without thinking about the consequences. It was only afterwards when I felt awful that regret would kick in. Make shielding a part of your daily routine because negative energy doesn't announce itself to you when it's on its way; it just shows up. But if you are prepared for it, it won't affect you. Here are some shielding exercises you can practice daily:

ZIPPER OF LIGHT

- Visualize your energy field being protected by a strong shield of light that is zipped around you tightly. There are no holes in the shield, so nothing can get in.

- Say out loud that this shield protects you against all negative energy that radiates from people, places, and things.

- Say out loud that any negative energy that comes in your direction will instantly be returned to sender before it has a chance to enter your orbit.

- Say out loud that you will not lose the love, positivity, and radiant energy flowing through you because it belongs to you, and your shield of light will make sure it stays with you.

Mirror Shielding

- Visualize a mirror wrapped around your body. The mirror part is on the outside, reflecting away from you.

- Any negative energy that comes your way will hit the mirror and go back to where it came from. You won't absorb any of it.

- Say out loud, "This mirror creates a barrier between me and all negative energy. It bounces off the mirror and goes back to where it came from."

- Keep this image in your mind for a few minutes.

- Come out of the visualization, take some deep breaths, and get on with your day.

Nature Grounding

- Go outside and find some grass.

- Whether you sit or stand, make sure your feet are flat on the ground beneath you.

- Visualize roots coming out of the bottom of your feet and going down into the earth. These roots have anchored you firmly to the ground.

- Imagine the roots pulling energy up from the ground and filling your body with protective, grounding energy.

- This energy is strong and unbreakable because it has come directly from the Earth's core. Imagine this energy forming a protective shield around you.

- Repeat this mantra out loud: "I am grounded and protected by the impenetrable energy from the earth. No negative energy can get through this shield."

- Keep this image in your head, and repeat the mantra until you feel fully protected and grounded.

- **Create Distance:** Let's say you woke up late and you didn't get to do the things you normally do to protect your energy. You run into a friend at a coffee shop and she wants to have a quick chat. You quickly discover that she wants to complain about her boyfriend, which is fine. Let her talk, but create distance between yourself and her emotions so you don't absorb them. You can do this by visualizing yourself taking a step back from her emotions. Think of yourself either taking a few steps back while she is speaking, or imagine being swallowed up by a large bubble. You can still hear her speaking, but the bubble is protecting you from her energy. Don't be afraid to practice this distancing technique. It won't mean you can't empathize with the person—you just won't absorb their energy, which means you free yourself from carrying their pain.

- **Take a Break:** If you are in an environment where there is a lot of negative energy floating around, take a break. This could be at work, or at a social event. When you start feeling the negative energy, go outside, take a walk, and do some deep breathing exercises. Repeat mantras to help you shake off the negative energy, such as:

- "I refuse to allow other people's emotions to control me."
- "I release all negative energy that does not belong to me."
- "I am a beacon of light and positivity; therefore, other people's negative energy is not welcome here."
- "Embracing peace comes naturally to me because I am protected against all negative energy."
- "My inner peace cannot be disturbed by negative energy from other people."
- "I am surrounded by uplifting and positive energy."
- "I let go of everything that is weighing me down."
- "My mind is clear and my spirit is calm."
- "I am a vessel of compassion and love. Negative energy does not belong here."

When you feel better, go back inside and have fun with your friends and family. But take as many breaks as you need to because sometimes, negative energy can sneak up on you even if you got rid of it the first time around.

- **Ask Yourself:** When you arrive home from work or a social event and your emotions are all over the place, ask yourself whether those emotions belong to you or if you've picked them up from someone else during the day. To determine whether they belong to you, think about whether anything happened to you directly that has affected your emotions.

Did a co-worker do something to annoy you? Did you have an unsuccessful meeting with your manager? Did your partner start an argument with you over text? If you haven't had any personal negative experiences throughout the day, you can safely say that the emotions you are carrying don't belong to you, and you can freely release them without feeling guilty. To release someone else's emotions, make the following statement: "These emotions don't belong to me, and I choose to reject them completely." Keep repeating this statement until you can no longer feel the negative emotions you have absorbed.

If you are used to living a life where you are constantly giving pieces of yourself away, it is going to feel very uncomfortable practicing healthy selfishness. Not only are people going to make you feel guilty for putting yourself first, but you will find it hard to put yourself first—which is why it will be easy for people to make you feel guilty. This is why it's so important to have the right people in your life. Toxic people don't care about your well-being as long as their needs are met. They will see you struggling and step right on over you to get to where they need to go. A lot of you reading this have toxic people in your life, but now it's time to weed them out. Find out how to do this in Chapter 7.

LET THEM GO: HOW TO GET RID OF TOXIC PEOPLE AND IDENTIFY AND NURTURE HEALTHY RELATIONSHIPS

When you decide to change your life, you will need to make a lot of sacrifices. Personal development requires you to invest time and energy into doing the work required to become the best version of yourself. You are going to be extremely excited about your new goals, and the first thing you will do is start telling the people closest to you about what you hope to achieve over the next few years. You tell them because you expect them to share your enthusiasm, but instead you will be met with an avalanche of negativity. This is because they are not ready to take the mental leap required to make the same changes in their life, although they want the success.

I used to be one of those people who had a love-hate relationship with celebrities. I was obsessed with their lifestyles because I wanted to live like them, but I also hated them for their success. When I would read about them spending millions of dollars on random items, I would say things like, "People are starving in the world and all these celebrities can think about is buying houses and cars—how selfish!" But the reality was that I was jealous and wished I had the means to do the same. I assumed the rich and famous just got lucky; I had no idea how hard they have worked to get to where they are, and how hard they continue to work to maintain their success. This is the mentality your friends will adopt when they see you making progress. They will want your lifestyle, but will not understand how hard you have worked to achieve it, and so, instead of congratulating you, they will demean you.

Also, the dynamics of your relationships will change. As mentioned, you will need to make a lot of sacrifices, which means you won't be able to spend as much time with friends and loved ones. Your biggest distractions will come from the people closest to you. Eventually, you will be forced to set boundaries, and it will be a problem. When you have always given your friends complete access to your life, and all of a sudden you have restricted that access, they are not going to go down without a fight, and you will experience a lot of resistance. The truth is that you will lose a lot of friends on this journey, but the good news is that you will gain many more. As difficult as it will be to let some of your friends go, you won't have much choice if you are serious about achieving your goals. Keep reading to find out how to let unhealthy friendships go and nurture the right ones.

ARE YOUR FRIENDS TOXIC?

I didn't know my friends were toxic, because *I* was toxic. But my transformation revealed how toxic my friends actually were, and I had to sever many ties to get to where I am today. Letting go of friendships isn't easy but it's necessary, so let's take a look at how to identify toxic friendships:

They Undermine You: It took a while for me to ditch the friends I needed to ditch, partly because I didn't have the courage to cut them off completely—even though deep down I knew that was what I needed to do. After I wrote my first book and it flopped, it was obvious that my friends were happy I had failed. The energy I got from them was, "Okay, now you can stop all this 'I'm going to become a world-class author' nonsense and come back to the land of 'We ain't going nowhere in life.'" But I hadn't given up, and I refused to allow them to kill my soul. But they were always throwing shade, and they did it in front of people too. One evening, a friend invited me to her work do, and so I went. When one of her colleagues asked what I did for a living, I said, "I'm a bookkeeper by day and an author by night." My friend quickly chimed in and said, "A failed author!" And then proceeded to tell her the story of how I wrote a book and thought I could publish it myself but it didn't quite work out as planned. I was both embarrassed and angry.

According to psychologists, when people do this, it's referred to as "social undermining." These small digs are designed to knock you off the high horse your attacker believes you've placed yourself on. If you are not strong-minded, you will start doubting yourself and feel as if your friends are not supporting you. Eventually, you will become bitter and resentful.

They Guilt-Trip You: Guilt-tripping involves making you feel bad for your success. They will take advantage of your empathetic nature, and when you share an accomplishment, they will say something like, "Must feel great not having to struggle while the little people like us are still trying to make it." Your friend will try and make you feel like the only reason they are unhappy is because you are successful. They will cast themselves as the victim of circumstance and subtly pressure you to hide your success.

Another way of guilt-tripping you is through passive-aggressive remarks or backhanded compliments. Instead of celebrating with you when something good happens, they will say something like, "What does it feel like to have things just land in your lap like that?" What they are really trying to say is that you don't work for your success—you just get lucky somehow. The aim of comments like this is to make you feel guilty for being proud of your accomplishments. They hope to chip away at your confidence and create an atmosphere where you don't feel comfortable sharing your wins.

They Waste Your Time: Time is the most valuable resource in the world because you can never get it back. Over the years, I have learned that very few people understand this concept. Those who don't have anything better to do with their time waste it, and they will waste yours too if you let them. Once I started trading the time I spent with friends for writing, they became increasingly more demanding. They knew I had started taking my life more seriously and could no longer come at me with the drama and gossip. Instead, they started asking me to help them get *their* lives together. At first, I was excited about this because I really did want to keep my friends. They would organize evenings where we would get together and do things like create vision boards, talk about our goals, and go to conferences about success. However, I quickly realized that they were not serious, because they were not implementing anything they were learning. The whole thing was a joke to them; they just wanted access to me and they knew the only way they could get it was to pretend they were on my level.

They Compete With You: I am all for healthy competition when everyone knows what's going on and a group of friends are just trying to better themselves. However, when competition is one-sided and fueled by insecurity and jealousy, it's a problem. Here are a few signs that your friend is competing with you:

- **They Enjoy Your Bad News:** You can spot a hater a mile off because they perk up when you talk about your bad news and are willing to have a long conversation with you about it. But when you share good news, they act as if they don't want to hear it. They will quickly change the subject because they don't want to hear about you doing well for yourself.

- **They Copy You:** They say that imitation is the best form of flattery, but your friend is not copying you to imitate you—they are copying you because they are in competition with you and they need to keep up. If you get your nails done, they will get theirs done; if you buy a new handbag, they'll buy one. A competitive friend will literally go broke trying to make sure they look better than you.

- **They Avoid Celebrating With You:** As mentioned, a competitive friend doesn't react well to your good news. When you want to celebrate your wins, even if it's something small, they'll have an excuse as to why they can't make it.

- **They Downplay Your Accomplishments:** Even if you won the Nobel Peace Prize, it would never be good enough for a competitive friend—although, deep down, they are jealous. Anytime you mention any of your successes, they will say things like, "That's not that much of a big deal. Anyone could have done it."

- **They Try to One-Up You:** Anything you do, they will try and do it better. Trying to one-up you is similar to copying you, but this is about doing it better. So, if you buy a new car, they'll buy a more prestigious one. If you go on vacation, they'll go on a more luxurious one. If you buy a four-bedroom house, they'll buy a five-bedroom one. You will know your friend is trying to one-up you because this is not a random occurrence—they do it all the time.

- **They Are Always Bragging:** There is a difference between sharing your success with your loved ones and bragging. Bragging involves showing off, seeking admiration and validation, and attempting to elevate yourself above others. The tone in which the success is mentioned is often self-centered and boastful. You will also find that when a person is bragging, it's inappropriate. It's usually right after you've mentioned good news, or they will cut you off partway through speaking to make their announcement.

- **They Keep Tabs on You:** A competitive friend is always trying to find out your next move so they can do it better. They will do things like spy on your through social media and keep asking you questions about what you are doing.

They Are Always Involved in Drama: Some of my friends were addicted to drama. If there was no drama, it was a bad day for them. Whether the drama was at work, home, or with a romantic partner, there was always something going on. And guess who they would call to discuss the drama? You guessed it—me! I would spend hours on the phone gossiping about foolishness. At that time, the problem was that I liked the drama. I got excited when my phone rang and I heard the words, "Hey, girl, let me give you the tea!" The drama was so juicy that it was better than watching an entire series of reality TV. I lived for it just as much as they did. But it didn't become a major distraction until I started working on my goals. Then it was like, *I really don't have time for this.*

There are underlying reasons why some people are always involved in drama, and one of them is that they don't have anything better to do with their time. Once you decide you want more out of life, drama will no longer interest you because you will be so focused on accomplishing your goals. Your mind will be filled with all the things you need to get done and not preoccupied with what's going on in other people's lives. When you get to this point, you will be forced to put boundaries up, but this won't go down well with your friends.

They Violate Boundaries: As mentioned, you won't realize your friends are toxic until you decide to change your life, and one sign of a toxic friend is that they violate your boundaries. I started off limiting my phone calls to half an hour a night. Before that, I could spend up to six hours on the phone. As soon as I got off work at 5:00 p.m., I was on the phone and I didn't get off it until I went to bed at around 11:00 p.m. When I started organizing my life and put a plan in place to write my book, I had to cut down my phone time, and for the schedule I had created, I decided thirty minutes a night was all I could spare. My friends were not impressed and couldn't understand why I didn't want to spend all my time speaking to them. They would tell me that I didn't need to spend so much time writing, that there was no point anyway because how did I know I was going to be successful? When I got off the phone after thirty minutes, whoever I was talking to would call back two hours later claiming they needed to speak to me urgently. There was never anything urgent about what they had to say.

To prevent them calling back after the thirty minutes, I would put my phone on "do not disturb," which meant when anyone rang, they couldn't get through. So guess what—they would turn up at my apartment claiming they were worried about me because they had tried to call but couldn't get through! Things got so ridiculous I was forced to block people. If anyone turned up at my apartment, I didn't answer the door. For the drastic changes I needed to make in my life, I had to take drastic action, and if that meant losing all my friends, then so be it. I was sick of my life and I wanted to live the life I had envisioned for myself. No amount of my friends throwing tantrums was going to make me give up my dreams. My mentality had shifted—I couldn't stay where I was. My thought process was, "If the people in my life can't get with the program, oh, well!"

"THE CRABS IN THE BUCKET" MENTALITY

I was deeply distressed when I started my self-development journey and my friends and family members started throwing shade at me. It was very subtle, but I caught it every time. They would say things like, "Do you really think your writing is that good you could quit your job and make a full-time living as an author?" Or, "Independent authors don't make any money. You're better off getting a publisher." When I became an Amazon bestselling author, I was told, "But Amazon is hardly the *New York Times*, is it?" Jackie warned me that this would happen, but I was hoping my friends would be different. In psychology, this behavior is referred to as "the crabs in the bucket" mentality.

If there is one crab in a bucket and it decides to get out, it will crawl to the top and escape without any trouble. However, if there are several crabs in a bucket and one tries to escape, the others will latch onto it to pull it back down. This happens instinctively because all of the crabs want to escape, and the crab on top is seen as something to grab onto to help them because there is nothing to grip onto on the sides of the bucket. The end result is that all the crabs fall back into the bucket and their fate is sealed.

A similar mentality is found in humans. It is an instinct that derives from fear and insecurity. It causes people to feel that those they know are not entitled to have something if they themselves can't have it too. You will find this behavior in the workplace, amongst families, in romantic relationships, and in platonic friendships. When one person starts heading towards success, the others will attempt to pull them back down to their level. This is not a physical pulling down, but a psychological one where the people on the bottom will launch attacks at the individual on the rise because they are now perceived as a threat. The aim is to destroy the person's self-esteem so they willingly give up on their pursuit of excellence. In extreme cases they may spread rumors and gossip to discredit the person's efforts and isolate them from the group.

The "crabs in the bucket" mentality is extremely toxic. Not only does it negatively affect the person being attacked, but the person doing the attacking is also psychologically damaging themselves. They become obsessed with jealousy and envy, which has a negative effect on their mental health. These people waste all their time and energy trying to pull others down when they could invest it in themselves.

Let's dig a little deeper into this dynamic. As mentioned, humans tend to associate with people who are on the same level as them because we feel a sense of belonging and equality. Deep feelings of anxiety set in when someone of the same status attempts to climb the social ladder. The sting of watching this ascent is even worse than seeing celebrities dripping with success, because they were never in our social group anyway. This is why many successful people say they get more support from strangers than family members and friends. The reality is that deep down, everyone wants to be successful. Your loved ones do want you to succeed—but what they don't want is for you to become successful before them, or to become more successful than them. When this happens, the relationship dynamic switches, and you are now seen as competition instead of a once-beloved friend or family member.

HOW TO DEAL WITH CRABS IN YOUR CIRCLE

Shake them off! Because it is so disheartening that your once-beloved group of friends or family members are now your archenemies, people tend to try and fight for the relationships. They will ignore the sly comments, turn up to events even though they were not invited, try and find out what they've done wrong so they can fix it, or beg and plead for things to go back to normal. Unfortunately, if you are surrounded by crabs, there is no going back to the way things were unless you come back down to the bottom of the bucket. People with a crab mentality don't have the ability to go after their dreams. They are content where they are, and you can't pull them up to your level. Imagine standing on top of a table and your best friend is standing on the floor. You reach down in an attempt to pull her up on top of the table, but gravity doesn't allow it, and you end up on the floor with her. Unfortunately, there are some friends you will need to remove from your circle. Cutting people off is a very difficult thing to do, but if you want to get anywhere in life, you don't have a choice. Here are some tips on how to get rid of the crabs in your circle:

Distance Yourself: Getting rid of toxic friends is no easy task because they are going to hang on for dear life. Therefore, start by distancing yourself in the hopes that they will get the message. Initially, I sent a group message stating that I was writing my book and needed to limit communication because talking to and texting them was taking up too much of my time. I mentioned earlier that this didn't go down well, but I stuck to my guns. Then I started rejecting invitations. We went out every Friday and Saturday night and went on vacation once a year. I turned down every last invite. I was indirectly letting them know that I was no longer interested in maintaining the friendships. I took this route, and I would advise you to take it too, because toxic people lack self-awareness; they are selfish and don't care about your feelings. Their only concern is that they continue having access to you, and they will achieve this by any means necessary. I discussed earlier how my former friends would violate my boundaries and keep calling me, despite me telling them I needed to limit my talking time to thirty minutes. Some of your toxic friends will eventually run out of patience and leave you alone. For others, you might need to block them. More on this later.

I had one friend, let's call her Linda, who wasn't overtly toxic, but she was a big distraction and extremely codependent. We lived in each other's pockets for many years. We were the type of friends where you would never see one without the other. We spent the whole day texting each other, we were on the phone during our lunch breaks, and on the phone again after work. When I started my self-development journey, she took it the hardest. I really did feel bad about ditching Linda, but it had to be done.

Linda became a major distraction, and that was when I realized I needed to sever our relationship. At first, I told her that I couldn't spend too much time on the phone because I needed to write. But she didn't understand what it was going to take for me to achieve my goals. She would blow up my phone with text messages and social media posts and then call me if I hadn't responded. I would let her know that I couldn't keep breaking my focus to text, and she would say, "Yeah, but you can just go back to your work after you've responded." But if she was sending me twenty texts a night, what time did I have left to write? She basically went from not cutting down our speaking time to replacing our conversations with text messages. So, then, I started putting my phone on "do not disturb." After I had finished writing, I was too exhausted to text her back, and would respond on my lunch break. This went on for months until she got her mom to contact my mom to find out what was going on. I had already given my mom the heads-up, so she just told her I was really busy at the moment and left it at that. Eventually, Linda stopped messaging me and the friendship fizzled out, but it took a couple of years for this to happen.

If distancing yourself doesn't work, you will need to have an honest conversation with your friends.

Have a Conversation: Stubbornness is one of the many characteristics of toxic people. They simply refuse to take no for an answer because, as far as they are concerned, you don't have the right to reject them. Since distancing yourself hasn't worked, now it's time to have a very frank conversation about why you can't continue with the friendship. Here's how to go about it:

- **Write it Down:** Start by writing down all the reasons you want to end the friendship—so that when you meet up with them, you won't forget what you wanted to say. When you've been friends with someone for a long time, it can be easy to get talking, have a fantastic conversation and then change your mind about ending the friendship. Turn up to your meeting armed with your notebook so you don't lose track of what you want to say. Even though your friend probably won't want to end the relationship, providing solid reasons for your decision will help them understand where you are coming from.

Finally, it's important to understand that, regardless of the reasons you give for ending the friendship, it might cause offense. Some people simply won't understand why you are being so extreme. They might accuse you of being dramatic or thinking you are better than everyone. It's okay for them to think this way. Don't try and convince them they are wrong—you will waste your time and energy.

- **Arrange a Meeting:** Ending a friendship face to face is difficult, but doing so over the phone or by text message isn't a good idea. Firstly, what you don't want is to come across as a coward; and secondly, a face-to-face meeting gives you the opportunity to provide closure and it gives your friend clarity. Being able to see a person's facial expressions and read their body language is essential for getting your point across effectively. Your friend might not take you seriously if you end the relationship over the phone.

  When you contact your friend, let them know you want to meet up for an important private conversation, to ensure they don't bring anyone else. Additionally, arrange to meet in a public place like a coffee shop or a park to reduce the chances of any emotional outbursts. Your friend might not like what you've got to say, and people are more likely to control their emotions when they are in public.

- **Prepare Yourself:** Although ending the friendship is your idea, this is a difficult conversation to have, so prepare yourself mentally beforehand. While you can never be all the way prepared because you don't know how they are going to react, when I had to end some of my friendships, I prepared myself mentally by doing the following:

- **Worst-Case Scenario:** I envisioned the worst thing that could possibly happen when ending the friendship. I played the scenario over in my mind and how I would react to it. This protected my mind from going down a rabbit hole of imagining what was going to happen, because I had already forced myself to do so.

- **Speak to Someone:** I spoke to my mentor Jackie when it was time to end some friendships. We had a deep conversation about what happens to your relationships when you decide to take your life seriously and become successful. It was comforting to know that she had been through a very similar situation and that her life significantly improved once she removed the energy drainers from her life.

- **Meditation:** Meditation is a powerful tool to help you prepare mentally and emotionally for a difficult conversation. I meditated for half an hour before leaving the house, and I felt calm, focused, and relaxed. Feeling this way definitely helped me get through the conversation more easily.

• **Active Listening:** After you've provided your reasons for ending the friendship, give your friend an opportunity to respond if they want to. Some will accept your position and leave it at that. Others will want to explain why you are wrong. Whatever they have to say, let them speak, and practice active listening. If they get irate (which they might), don't engage. You know you are doing the right thing because you've spent a lot of time thinking about it. It's probably harder for you than it is for them. Once your friend has expressed themselves fully, let them know you understand what they've said but that you don't intend on changing your mind.

- **Remain Hopeful:** Although the conversation ended with the door to the friendship officially closed because that's what you need for now, remain hopeful that one day, your friend will be ready to do the work required to change his/her life. While they will be upset in the moment, a few years down the line when they are on their own self-development journey and needing to end some friendships, they will remember your conversation and realize why you had to do it.

  After the conversation, give it a couple of weeks and see what happens. If they keep contacting you, block them. If a person is not willing to accept your wishes and how you feel about a situation, it's time to take extreme measures. If you see them out and about, be polite, say hello, and keep it moving. But I doubt you will see them again. When you switch paths, you rarely, if ever, bump into old acquaintances. I haven't, and it's been several years since I cut the cord. I'm sure some of them stalk me on social media, but that's their problem and not mine.

WHAT DO HEALTHY FRIENDSHIPS LOOK LIKE?

When you've been so used to toxic friendships, you are not going to know what healthy friendships look like. This is something I have had to learn over the years, and every so often, I will slip up and open the door to a toxic friend. But as soon as my discernment kicks in, I don't wait for them to start wreaking havoc in my life—I get rid of them immediately. It sounds harsh, but protecting my peace is one of my top priorities. Here is some insight into what a healthy friendship should look like:

Non-Judgmental: Nobody likes to be judged, but it's difficult to be non-judgmental when we all have our own opinions, likes, and dislikes that are strongly influenced by society. It's easy to think you are better than the person who chooses to live a life contrary to society's norms because it is frowned upon by society. For example, women who look down on other women for sleeping with multiple partners. Why do we have a problem with this? Because society says it's wrong. But if a woman wants to live her life like this, it shouldn't concern us. The same is true with your friendships. However, it's important to make a distinction between being honest and being judgmental.

An honest friend wants the best for you; therefore, when you are doing something that they feel is not in your best interests, they will tell you. On the other hand, a judgmental friend looks down on you for the things you do, and when they confront you about it, you will feel small and less than confident. A judgmental friend is controlling; they shame you into taking on their beliefs and values, and they refuse to respect your choices.

In my current friend group, I have Christian and Jewish friends. Religious people are often viewed as judgmental because they don't agree with certain lifestyles. Sometimes this assessment is justified because of how they go about letting people know they don't agree with their lifestyle. But my friends are not like that; they don't try and force their beliefs on us, or chastise us when they see us doing things that go against their beliefs. They have enough self-awareness to understand that people are entitled to their beliefs, and they are okay with that. However, there are certain things they don't participate in, and the non-religious people respect that too.

Supportive: Supportive friendships help you feel accepted for who you are; they motivate you, lift you up, and you know there is always a listening ear available when you need it. Care, respect, and shared affection are the main characteristics of supportive friendships. They are balanced in that there is an equal amount of give and take from all parties. You won't find yourself being the one making all the effort to maintain the friendship. You all understand each other, validate each other, and there is a sense of acceptance and belonging amongst you.

Supportive friendships are also characterized by reliability and loyalty. You are always there for each other during the good and the bad times providing the necessary emotional support. You can be vulnerable around supportive friends because they won't use it against you. Sharing your weaknesses, anxieties, and fears comes naturally. Doing so deepens the emotional bond you have with each other. You don't fear being open and honest with each other because you have all created a healthy environment in which you can do so.

Supportive friendships contribute to our mental health, happiness, and quality of life. A 2017 study published in the National Library of Medicine found that social support helps to decrease depression and stress, and boosts physical health and self-confidence.

Respect Boundaries: Everyone needs boundaries in their relationships. However, HSPs and empaths need stronger boundaries because, due to their empathetic nature, people tend to take advantage of them. Boundaries are essential for maintaining healthy friendships; they provide a strong foundation for clear communication, respect, and understanding—all of which are essential elements for healthy relationships. When enforced and maintained in the right way, boundaries create a natural balance between individuality and closeness in friendships. They provide space for both parties to express their feelings and thoughts openly, discuss shared experiences, and support each other, while maintaining their independence and unique identities.

In order for friendships to thrive, they need balance. When people live inside each other's pockets, it becomes stifling, doesn't provide room for growth, and leads to codependent relationships. On the flip side, a lack of emotional bonding and extreme separatism creates superficial and distant friendships. Boundaries assist in working your way around this delicate balance.

HOW TO MAKE NEW FRIENDS

Out with the old, and in with the new! One thing I discovered when it came to making new friends was that it was hard. Most adults already have their friend groups and they've usually been friends for years. I had known all of my old friends since high school; they were all I knew and it was really hard to end those friendships. But I knew I had to if I was going to achieve my goals. When I tried making new friends, it got to a point where I just thought it wasn't worth it. Most of the women I met were not really interested in adding another friend to their roster because they already had so many. Not only that, they were also either married or in long-term relationships, and they had kids. But I refused to give up, and I eventually made a really nice group of friends. Here are some of the things I did to meet like-minded people:

Improve Your Social Skills: Once you get settled into life, you forget about social skills. You've got your friends, you might have a partner, and your career is going well. You have been fully accepted by the people you surround yourself with the most, so the last thing on your mind is improving your social skills. But I can tell you that it helps. I was very rusty when I first started trying to make new friends, and I believe one of the reasons I wasn't very successful was because my social skills were trash. I felt a bit awkward in new environments, I wasn't the best conversationalist, and I just kind of sat around hoping other people would make the effort. I didn't start seeing results until *I* made an effort, though, and that came in the form of improving my social skills.

I'm an introvert so I found this particularly difficult, and one of the things I hate the most is small talk. Oh, my goodness—I'd rather not talk at all than discuss the weather or some other annoying random subject. But that's how people converse; it's social etiquette—and if I wanted to make new friends, I had to play the game. So, I got on the Internet and watched a ton of videos about improving your social skills, and I also read a lot of books. I found these to be the most helpful:

- *How to Win Friends & Influence People: The Only Book You Need to Lead You to Success* by Dale Carnegie

- *Conversationally Speaking: Tested New Ways to Increase Your Social and Personal Effectiveness* by Amanda Goodwin Caporaletti & Alan Garner

- *Improve Your Social Skills* by Daniel Wendler

- *How to Talk to Anyone: 92 Little Tricks for Big Success in Relationships* by Leil Lowndes

- *Charming Your Way to the Top: Hollywood's Premier P.R. Executive Shows You How to Get Ahead* by Michael Levine

Make the First Move: One way to make new friends is to join a club or start a hobby. Instead of waiting around for people to talk to you, approach them first, because there's a high chance they are just as reluctant as you to walk up to random individuals and start talking.

Make the First Phone Call: After getting the contact details of the people you meet, instead of poking them on social media, which is a common practice after meeting someone new, develop a connection by making the first phone call.

Make Friends Online: I'm an advocate for making friends online because I've made several and we are still good friends to this day. There are plenty of online groups you can join where making friends is the main goal. Typically, what happens in these groups is that once you get to know each other, the friendships continue offline. You will be amazed at how much fun you can have in these online groups. Nevertheless, when meeting new people, always do so in a public place where there are a lot of bystanders. Don't invite random individuals to your house until you feel completely safe. Unfortunately, there are a lot of bad people in the world.

How to Nurture Your New Relationships

At first, I found making new friends similar to networking. You go out to all these events, collect a load of business cards, follow a bunch of new people on social media—and then nothing. You don't hear from each other again, and when you do bump into them at another networking event, they don't remember you. I once made a friend at a pottery class. We exchanged contact information and didn't contact each other. A few months later, we met again at the same class, and she spoke to me as if she was meeting me for the first time. Now, I could put it down to amnesia or a mental illness, but

I'd be more inclined to state that she's met so many people that she just forgot. Needless to say, we never became friends.

If you want to be an effective networker, you've got to follow up. Friendships work the same way. Don't sit around waiting for people to contact you—be the initiator. However, it's also important to remember that friendships are a team effort; if your new friends are not making an effort, you'll need to ditch them too. You can't be the one always making phone calls and arranging the meetups. After a while, you will get into a rhythm with the people you are destined to remain friends with, and the friendship will flow naturally. Nevertheless, here are some tips to maintain your new friendships:

Make Time: If you don't make time for your new friendships, they won't flourish. You will never get past the superficial level of associates. If you want real friendships, making time for them is essential. Outside of the social aspect, studies have found that people who spend more time with their friends cope with stress better. Instead of relying on unhealthy coping mechanisms like drugs and alcohol, they talk things out with their friends. Additionally, people with strong support systems are more emotionally stable and they feel better about themselves and life in general.

Commit to Something: Set a date in the diary that works for everyone and stick to it. Whether you meet up for dinner, go bowling, or meet up at each other's houses, when you commit to a date, it takes the pressure off not knowing when you are going to meet up again. Everyone is on the same page and you can look forward to seeing each other once every month, or every three months, or however you choose to do it. It's okay if you or someone else in the group can't make it—things happen, from sickness to family problems. As long as you communicate with each other, you'll be fine. And that brings me to my next point.

Communicate: Unfortunately, most people have terrible communication skills. Off topic, but I personally believe that's the underlying reason why many marriages end in divorce. Statistics state that the top three reasons for divorce are falling out of love, money problems, and personal problems. Each one of these problems could have been resolved if both parties knew how to communicate their needs to each other effectively.

However, when I started making new friends, I found we were all on our personal development journeys and improving our communication skills was something we were working on. This made developing our relationships a whole lot easier.

It's important to understand that healthy relationships do not just magically appear out—they are built. The process of building a healthy relationship requires a certain level of vulnerability so our friends can gain a better understanding of us. That vulnerability is expressed through communicating with each other. Effective communication invites the person you are communicating with into your inner world. It allows you to share important pieces of information that help them understand your emotional needs. They gain insight into what makes you happy, sad, angry, etc. When people feel heard, seen, understood, and supported, they open up more and the friendship deepens.

Be Present: I went to a friend's wedding a few months back, and in the invitation there was a letter banning any recording or photography of the wedding with phones or any other digital equipment. The inviters went on to explain that they wanted their guests to be fully present without the distraction of technology. They also stated that there was going to be a professional cameraman and a photographer, and everyone would receive video footage and photographs after the wedding. I was in total agreement with their policy because at the wedding I had been to before that, every single person had their phone out recording the entire ceremony. There was also a professional cameraman, and when I received the video footage, it looked ridiculous—everyone was watching the ceremony through their phones!

Being present with your friends is important. You don't want to miss the moments that matter. If you're too focused on capturing images for social media, or your mind is in a thousand different places at once, you're not present. Here are some tips on how to be more present when you meet up with friends:

- **Put Your Phone Away:** One thing I can't stand is to have a conversation with a person while they're on their phone. I think it's extremely rude and disrespectful. Like, I get it—everyone is totally addicted to their phones these days; however, burying your head in your phone when talking to someone shows you're not really interested in what the other person has to say. I compare it to a man walking hand in hand with his girlfriend, a hot chick walks by, and he literally forgets he's with his girlfriend. Even though he's still holding her hand, he stares at this other woman, and then, when she walks past, cranes his neck to continue checking her out. He's basically saying, "I've got a girlfriend but I'm not that into her because I have the audacity to admire other women when she's in my presence." To some, this might sound like an extreme comparison—but trust me, it's not. The next time you're having a conversation with someone and they are submerged in their phone, ask them if they're listening to you. I guarantee they'll say yes. But when you ask them to repeat what you said, they'll say, "Run that by me again." In other words, they were not listening.

When you meet up with your friends, I suggest having a "no phones" rule where everyone puts their phone in their bag so you are all fully present. I understand that there can be emergencies, but with today's technology, you can change your ring tone and messaging to an emergency sound so you know when something serious is going on.

- **Make Eye Contact:** Whether you're having a one-on-one conversation, or one person is speaking to the group, always make eye contact with the person you are speaking to. You might not think eye contact is that important when talking to your friends because they know you, they trust you, and they don't mind if you keep looking away because they know you don't have anything to hide. While this is true, making eye contact runs deeper than the trust factor. For one, it shows you are listening; it shows you are empathetic and have a desire to understand the speaker's perspective. Making eye contact also shows you are attentive, engaged, and that you want to take your connection further. Also, you will get to know your friend better by making eye contact because you will notice their emotional expressions, which gives you additional insight into how they feel.

- **Active Listening:** Listening is a skill, and most people are not very good at it. A survey by Accenture Research found that ninety-six percent of respondents believed they were good listeners. But this statistic was contradicted by a study published in *Scientific American* magazine that discovered that we only retain half of the information a person tells us, and that's directly after they've said it. So why are we such terrible listeners? Firstly, it's not something we are taught. The last time I checked, parents were not teaching their children to be active listeners. They want them to listen long enough so they do what they say, and that's about it. Neither is active listening a class we take in school. In general, people listen in order to respond—we would rather be heard than listen. And that's a problem.

Active listening ensures you are fully present when listening to someone. It helps you to completely engage with the speaker so you can gain a better understanding of what they are saying. Here's how to practice active listening:

- **Nonverbal Cues:** Another reason eye contact is so important is that it allows you to pay attention to body language. As mentioned, people say more with their unconscious movements than they do with their words. During a serious conversation, when a person's body language contradicts what they are saying, it could be a cry for help, so pay attention.

- **No Interrupting:** Have you ever had a conversation with someone who is continuously trying to finish your sentences or interrupting to tell you about something similar that happened to them? They will usually use the classic phrase, "Not to cut you off but..." Oh, my goodness, it's so annoying—but we are all guilty of it. Don't say anything when a person is speaking. Use your body language to show you are listening.

- **No Conclusions:** When you jump to conclusions, not only are you wrong most of the time, but it hints that the speaker is taking too long to get their point across, and you want them to hurry up and say what they're saying because you've got better things to do than listen to their long-winded story. This might not be the case at all; the story might be so exciting that you can't wait to hear the end of it. Nevertheless, wait until they have finished speaking before chiming in.

- **No Mental Planning:** I can be having a conversation with someone and thinking about a number of different things, from what I'm going to have for dinner, to an appropriate response to what the person is saying. Clear your mind during a conversation and focus completely on what the person is saying.

- **No Imposing:** Someone can be midway through what they are saying and the listener is already offering their opinion and providing solutions. Don't say anything until the person has finished speaking, to ensure you have a full understanding of what they are saying. Additionally, the speaker might not want your opinion or a solution—they just want someone to listen to them.

- **Stay Focused:** I wonder what the people I used to speak to before I improved my listening skills thought of me when we spoke, because I was all over the place. If someone walked into the room, I would look in that direction; if the noise level went up, I'd look in that direction; I would look through my bag for stuff, smooth down my clothes—the list goes on and on. I was terribly unfocused during conversations. Stay focused during a conversation by doing all the things mentioned above.

- **Ask Questions:** Once the person has finished speaking, if you feel like you need more information before responding, ask questions. If you feel you haven't fully understood what the person was saying, ask a question like, "When you said XYZ, what exactly did you mean by that?" Or, "I don't think I quite understood what you meant by XYZ. Can you explain it again please?" Some people are afraid to ask questions because they don't want the speaker to think they were not listening. But it actually does the opposite—asking questions shows you are interested in what the person has to say and that you have a desire to understand them better.

- **Summarize:** Once the speaker has said what they want to say, make sure you have fully understood everything that was said by summarizing the conversation. If you've misinterpreted something, the speaker will let you know.

- **Show Up:** Showing up doesn't mean making grand gestures all the time. In fact, it's often the small details that are appreciated the most. Here are some small ways you can show up for your friends:

  - Send inspirational messages of encouragement once a week.

  - Remember their kids', close relatives', or loved one's birthdays.

  - Make the effort to call your friends at least twice a month, even if it's just for fifteen minutes.

  - Show an interest in the lives of the people they love the most.

  - When you see something nice such as a social media post, or you read something in a book, or see something in a magazine, send it to your friend and say why it reminded you of them.

- Pay attention to the things they want and need. A friend might say, "I wish I had a teapot like that." If you're able to, buy it as a random gift.

- Be on time when you meet up. I know life can get hectic, but being on time is important, especially when you don't have much time to spare.

- Listen to them, even if you're not really interested in what they're saying.

- Tell your friends why they mean so much to you.

- Ask questions so you can get to know them better.

- Celebrate their wins with them, even the small ones.

- Hug your friends when you see them.

- Cook for your friends every once in a while.

- Offer to look after the kids so they can spend time with their partner.

- Keep your word at all times unless it's an absolute emergency.

- If you ever get into an argument, admit your mistake and apologize before things get out of hand.

Finally, it's important to mention that changing friend groups or keeping people at arm's length doesn't mean you think you are better than them, although that's what they will assume. You are just traveling on a different path that they are not ready to take. Everyone evolves in their own time, and some people never evolve. The bottom line is you can't allow others to hold you back because it's not *their* season for elevation. If they catch up, great—if not, keep it moving!

Before you flip the page, I want to ask you a question. What is your truth? I've asked this question to hundreds of people over the years, and the most common answer is, "I don't know." Knowing your truth is essential to living an authentic and unapologetic life. In the next chapter, I will teach you how to define your truth and stand in it.

CHAPTER 8:

AUTHENTIC LIVING: TAP INTO THE POWER OF STANDING IN YOUR TRUTH

I f I was to ask you if you considered yourself a liar, you would probably say no, and so would the majority of the people I asked. Apparently, society hates liars because they are deemed untrustworthy. Before being questioned in court, we are required to place our right hand on the Holy Bible and swear to tell the truth. Why? Because lying is unacceptable—right? But the world we live in encourages us to lie to ourselves and to others because if we don't conform to the norms and values that have been established for us, we are judged and ridiculed. We see what happens to people who stand in their "unconventional" truth, and since we have no desire to experience the same fate, we conform. This is especially true for women. We are expected to get married and start a family by a certain age. But those who opt for an alternative lifestyle, such as to remain single and childfree, are called selfish, bitter, and every name under the sun. Why can't people live their truth in peace? I lived society's truth for most of my life and I was miserable. Now that I stand in my own truth, I am happier than I have ever been—and I want you to have the same experience. In this chapter, I am going to teach you how to find your truth and stand in it.

How to Find Your Truth

Before you learn how to stand in your truth, let's define it. Standing in your truth means embracing your values and beliefs, and living in a way that's true to you without fear. It requires you to be honest with yourself and everyone you associate with. Here are the main elements of what is required to stand in your truth:

Self-Awareness: Standing in your truth requires you to know exactly who you are. You can achieve this by engaging in continuous introspection and self-reflection so you have a clear understanding of what truly matters to you.

Authenticity: Being true to yourself is at the heart of standing in your truth. This means refusing to conform to societal expectations that have been placed on you if they don't align with your truth. When you live an authentic life, you accept your identity and express yourself freely, regardless of whether people agree with you or not.

Honesty: Honesty is essential for standing in your truth because you must remain truthful and transparent with yourself and others even if they don't adhere to the same truths. Dishonesty leads to you hiding behind falsehoods and deceptions that ultimately lead to you compromising your truth.

Integrity: Have you ever met someone whose behavior changes depending on their environment? This is a person who either doesn't know their truth, or doesn't have the courage to stand in it. You need integrity to stand in your truth or you will compromise your beliefs to appease others. Integrity also means making the right choices when you are faced with difficult decisions that don't align with your truth.

Courage: As mentioned, we live in a world in which people are ridiculed and ostracized for refusing to conform to the norms and values of society. Therefore, it takes courage to stand in your truth. Even if your truth is not considered "controversial," you will run into people who don't agree with you and disrespectfully oppose your truth. Your courage comes from having confidence in who you are and what you believe in, and it enables you to remain firm in your beliefs despite the rejection and criticism you face.

Boundaries: Your truth belongs to you because not everyone is going to agree with it. Unfortunately, some people don't have the emotional maturity to respect your truth and keep it moving. You will need to set boundaries with these individuals to protect yourself from being constantly undermined by them.

Now you have a better understanding of what it means to stand in your truth, it's time to find yours. As mentioned, I spent the majority of my life living someone else's truth because I had never thought about it. Deep down, I knew something was missing, but when you have been programmed to live a certain way, and everyone around you has conformed to that programming, you just fall in line until you get sick and tired of being sick and tired. People don't typically pick up self-help books until they get to this point, so I'm guessing that's where you are now.

Here are ten questions to ask yourself, to find your truth:

1. **What do I believe in? What are my core values?**
   Consider the principles that influence your decisions and actions. What are the things that matter the most to you?

2. **What pursuits and activities make me feel the most alive and fulfilled?**
   When do you feel the most joyful? Are these pursuits and activities what you are truly passionate about?

3. **When do I feel I am being my authentic self?**
   Think about the people you are with, and the environments you are in where you can be your authentic self without feeling as if you are being judged.

4. **What are my strengths and talents?**
   What abilities and skills do you have that make you different from others? Being confident about your strengths and talents allows you to make meaningful contributions.

5. **What doubts and fears prevent me from living my truth?**
   Are you afraid of being judged? That you will lose friends? Or that you won't fit in when you start living your truth? Acknowledging these fears and doubts will help you overcome them.

6. **What causes do I have a desire to advocate for?**
   The causes that you are prepared to advocate for will reveal the things you truly care about.

7. **How do I define happiness and success for myself?**
   What does happiness and success look like to you outside of societal expectations?

8. **How has my past shaped who I am today?**
   What situations or events in your past have shaped who you are today? It's important to acknowledge these things because if they were negative, and they've shaped who you are in a negative way, you will need to do some internal work to overcome the hurt and pain these situations caused.

9. **How do I want to make an impact in the world?**
   You can only make an impact in the world when you know what you are passionate about. Your passion is your truth, and that's what makes you impactful.

10. **What steps do I need to take to start living my truth?**
   Identify the things you need to do to start living your truth. You might need to get around more people who share the same passions as you, or change your career. Whatever you need to do, start doing it now.

Now you've asked yourself these questions, I'm hoping you've found your truth. If so, congratulations. However, now that you've found your truth, it's essential that you respect everyone else's truth. I say this because this self-help journey is a trip, and sometimes it can cause you to become arrogant. That's what happened to me; I felt that, because I was learning all this new information and it was working for me, everyone else should abandon where they were going and jump on my train. I had to learn to respect everyone's truth—and here's why:

The Importance of Respecting Everyone's Truth

We live in an absolutely crazy world, and the Internet has exposed just how insane this world really is. When I first started writing, I knew I had to get online if I was going to sell any books. But I resisted it for a long time because I didn't want to deal with being publicly criticized. Everyone has an opinion about everything. There is nothing wrong with having an opinion—the problem is when we vilify others for not sharing our opinion. The Internet has opened the door to a lot of vile, hateful behavior because cowards can sit behind computer screens and bash people for expressing beliefs that don't align with theirs. I didn't want to become a target to such people and so I didn't have an online presence for a while. I'll be the first to admit that I'm guilty of turning my nose up to people I don't agree with; however, I also know that it's very ignorant of me and so I try not to do it. I've also come to the revelation that you reap what you sow, and if I want people to respect my truth, I must also respect theirs.

Nevertheless, as much as I try to respect everyone's truth, it's not easy. When a person has a completely different belief system to you, their thought process can seem illogical, and this can lead to an argument. Sometimes we don't like hearing a different opinion because we take it as a personal attack, even if it has nothing to do with us. When this happens, all reason and logic vanish, and the only thing we are left with is resentment. It then turns into a battle to prove who is right.

Here are some reasons why it's important to respect everyone's truth, whether you agree with it or not:

It Opens Your Eyes: Society would never progress if everyone thought the same, because we wouldn't challenge anything. We would still be living in the stone age if someone hadn't challenged why they did things that way and asked how they could make life easier. It is essential to think outside the box to expand your mental capacity and the world around you. As much as society expects us to conform to certain norms and standards, we are individuals, and we all have our own personal truths. These truths are born out of our experiences, values, and beliefs, and because we all experience life differently, our truths will be different. The human existence is exceptionally diverse. Take culture, for example. In one country, you can have several different cultures due to immigration. You might not understand someone else's culture, but that doesn't mean it's inferior to yours. By asking questions and finding out the meaning behind certain behaviors, you will grow to appreciate that culture. The same is true for truth; engaging in a meaningful conversation with a person who doesn't share the same truth as you will give you insight into why they believe the things they do.

Additionally, respecting someone's truth encourages personal growth because it gives you the opportunity to challenge your beliefs and assumptions. When you are exposed to ideologies that differ from yours, you are prompted to reflect on your perspective and think about new possibilities. By engaging in critical thinking and introspection, we learn to appreciate how complex human thoughts and experiences truly are.

Everyone Is Entitled to Their Truth: As mentioned, we live in a world where people will want to fight you if you don't agree with them. Influencers with strong or unconventional truths receive death threats because they won't fall in line with the status quo. It's ridiculous, but that's the way things are. You might not agree with someone's truth, but the reality is that everyone has the right to their own opinion. Most of you reading this live in a democratic society, and freedom of speech is the cornerstone of democracy. Open dialogue should be encouraged and not shut down because we don't agree. Having the right to an opinion is basic human dignity; we are all autonomous beings capable of thinking independently. Claiming that someone doesn't have the right to their opinion is stripping them of their human dignity. What you are implying is that they don't have the right to contribute meaningfully to society.

A lot of people are scared to share their truth because they are afraid of being judged. Unless that truth breaks the law, that shouldn't be the case. We should view it as a privilege to hear other people's truths because it helps broaden our understanding of the world. When people feel confident to share their perspectives, it encourages a rich exchange of ideas, which is important for societal and intellectual development.

Finally, allowing everyone to express their truths freely and live in their truth is essential to protecting those in the minority and promoting social justice. If you look back in history, things like slavery and the oppression of women would never have ended had people decided to keep their opinions to themselves. Unfortunately, those opinions were challenged and blood was shed in order for the oppressed to gain their rights and function like everyone else in society. The most recent movement is for the LGBTQ+ community to gain their full human rights. Without people voicing their opinions, there is no change.

At the end of the day, we can't hide under our individual rocks and expect to live fruitful lives. We've all got to coexist in this world. We work with people, sit next to people on the bus, buy from people, and hire people who have different truths from ours. It's all about respect and learning how to navigate these differences. I once had an hour-long conversation with a Sikh; he was a young man, very passionate about his religion. I listened politely and learned a lot about a different religion. I respected him for having a belief system and for having the boldness to share it, because, as mentioned, most people are afraid to do so in case they are judged.

It Gives People Courage: No one should be afraid to stand in their truth, but a lot of people are, because society has made it clear that alternative viewpoints are unacceptable. This has created a culture of insecurity where people don't feel confident living their authentic lives, and so they will only do so in spaces where they feel comfortable. A person who stands in their truth is clear about their values and beliefs. They don't fear rejection or judgment, because these beliefs and values have grounded them, which is why they have such a strong belief system. They have seen how powerfully their belief system works in their lives; therefore, they refuse to compromise. However, for someone who is new to standing in their truth, the rejection can knock their confidence. Each time you respect another person's truth, you boost their confidence and empower them to stand in it.

A More Peaceful World: We live in a world filled with a mixture of cultures, traditions, beliefs, and perspectives. One of the reasons there is so much conflict is because we refuse to respect others people's truths. Some individuals refuse to accept that truth is subjective, and that what is truth to one person will not be truth to another. Our truths have been shaped by our upbringing, culture, personal experiences and more. Acknowledging this diversity would lead to a massive reduction in conflict. Many disagreements, whether at the interpersonal, community, or international level, come about because of a refusal to accept different viewpoints. When people insist that their truth is correct, and everyone else's is wrong, it creates the foundation for hostility. But when people make the conscious choice to respect the beliefs and experiences of others, it opens the door to cooperation and shuts the door to confrontation.

Respecting differing truths also encourages empathy, where people are able to walk in another person's shoes and gain a deeper understanding of their perspectives and emotions. In this way, we validate their experiences and feelings. Through the emotional connection developed through acceptance, the bridge of division collapses, and individuals start becoming more aware of how their actions impact the lives of others, which leads to a more peaceful environment.

I am not saying we will solve all of the world's problems by respecting each other's truths, but if every individual in the world was to practice this principle, the world would definitely become a more peaceful place.

How to Respect Other People's Truths

Respecting how a person chooses to live their life doesn't mean you agree with them. You can disagree with something without being disrespectful. That said, you can show that you respect someone else's truth by doing the following:

Acknowledge: There are many versions of the truth, but that doesn't necessarily mean that truth is subjective. It means we have a different perspective to the truth we are being exposed to. Therefore, it comes as no surprise that everyone has their own version of the truth.

Validate: A common mistake people make when someone is speaking their truth and they don't agree is to shut them down. They interrupt and proceed to give them all the reasons why their truth is inaccurate. Instead of shutting someone down when you don't agree, allow them to speak their truth and let them know they have every right to believe in their truth. Leave it at that. There is no need to engage in a back-and-forth when you don't agree with something.

Accept: Even the greatest philosophers and thinkers don't know everything, so what makes you think that *you* do? The world's knowledge is so vast that there is no way anyone can know *everything*, regardless of how high their IQ is. Therefore, allow others to stand in their truth without challenging them. You might find that you learn something new.

How to Stand in Your Truth

Author Anne Dennish once said, "Stand in your truth with strength, kindness and compassion; anything less brings nothing more." Basically, standing in your truth is the only thing that will bring you true joy. It's not easy to do because, as mentioned, society expects you to conform to their norms. But I believe everyone reading this book is a non-conformist and you are ready to stand in your truth, despite the opposition you might face. Here are some tips that will help you to stand firmly in your truth:

Communicate Openly: When I started this truth journey, one of the things I decided to cut out of my life was excessive drinking and clubbing. I was tired of spending the weekend recovering from a hangover and putting myself in environments that did not uplift my soul. I remember the first time I told my friends I wouldn't be going out drinking with them anymore. You would have thought I'd delivered the most horrifying news, with the response I got. I explained exactly why I felt this way and asked if they could please respect my decision. I was still open to doing things like going out to dinner and the movies, but I was totally done with the clubbing and drinking. After chastising me for being boring and turning into a nun, every week, they proceeded to invite me out. My rejections were met with a barrage of insults that got worse after they'd had a few drinks. When we would meet up for dinner or some other outing, they ostracized me; they would intentionally only have conversations about their drunken nights out, knowing I couldn't join in because I wasn't there. I think their plan was to punish me until I changed my mind, but I never did. What I changed my mind about was our friendship! How about that!

Communicating your truth will ensure that everyone understands your position. Unfortunately, as you've just read about *my* friends, people will attempt to get you to compromise your truth—which is a form of boundary violation. If they continue to violate your boundaries, you are well within your rights to enforce the consequences. However, people are not mind readers; you can't expect others to respect your truth if they don't know what it is. I've met people like this—they will throw a hissy fit when individuals don't fall in line with an agenda that was never communicated.

Align Your Actions and Values: We've all heard the saying, "Actions speak louder than words," which is a very true statement. The majority of people know how to talk a good game, but they struggle to live it. Take goal-setting, for example. I was very good at talking about my goals, but actually doing the work to achieve them was an impossible task. I got there in the end, but it took a lot of work.

After watching several of my former friends raise their kids, I learned that children don't listen to what you say—they watch what you do, and that's what they emulate. I had a friend who constantly complained that her son outright refused to make his bed in the mornings. She said she was trying to teach him to be self-disciplined. Just before I was about to move into my house, I stayed at her home for a week. Every morning, she would raise hell with her son about making his bed, but she never made hers. It was then that I connected the dots—her son had no respect for her. It made no sense to his tiny four-year-old mind that the adult in his life could instruct him to do something that she herself didn't do. I'm not one for interfering with how people choose to raise their kids, but that stuck with me.

Basically, if you are going to take yourself seriously, and if you want people to take you seriously, make sure your actions align with your values. Now, I understand that no one is perfect, and you're not going to get it right all of the time. There will be days when, for whatever reason, you just can't get it right. However, when you fall, get back up. I live by this Chinese proverb, which really helps me out when I'm struggling: "Fall down seven times, stand up eight." In other words, never give up—no matter how many times you fall, keep moving forward.

Embrace Vulnerability: Contrary to popular belief, vulnerability is not a weakness. In fact, it takes an exceptionally strong person to be vulnerable. It involves surrendering to uncomfortable situations, which is essential if you are going to stand in your truth because, remember, not everyone is going to accept it.

Embracing vulnerability requires you to live a genuine life and be true to yourself. It means acknowledging that you have fears and insecurities, and that you are not perfect. Instead of hiding behind a mask, you choose to reveal your vulnerabilities. This authenticity makes it easier to stand in your truth because you have accepted every aspect of yourself. This provides you with a strong foundation for integrity and honesty, which are important elements of standing in your truth.

Vulnerability also helps improve your relationships. When you are honest about how you really feel, you encourage others to do the same. When two people are vulnerable, intimacy and trust deepen. When you reveal your genuine self, people are more likely to make a stronger connection with you. Authentic connections provide you with the support system you need in order to remain committed to standing in your truth. When loved ones support you, they make it easier for you to keep being authentic.

People shy away from standing in their truth because of fear. They are afraid of judgment, rejection, or that they won't have the strength to stand in their truth. Being vulnerable requires you to confront your fears. By doing so, you weaken their power over you and prevent them from dictating your choices and actions. Vulnerability builds resilience and enables you to confidently stand in your truth regardless of the opposition you might face.

Allowing yourself to be vulnerable opens the door to new learning opportunities and experiences. You free yourself from your rigid nature and expand your mind, allowing you to flourish and grow. Self-improvement further motivates you to stand in your truth because the more confident you become, the less likely you will be to compromise your beliefs and values.

Innovation and creativity thrive when people are vulnerable. Another aspect of vulnerability is that you become less afraid of judgment and failure. This gives you the courage to express yourself and explore new ideas without holding back. Creative freedom is essential for standing in your truth because it allows you to make meaningful contributions that reflect who you truly are.

Keep the Right Company: Your truth is your truth. There are some people who will agree with it, and there are some people who won't. In Chapter 7, you read about getting rid of toxic relationships.

The same applies when it comes to standing in your truth. At the moment, I have an amazing diverse group of friends, and we don't all hold the same beliefs. But despite our differences, our friendships are strong because we respect each other's truths. In life, you are constantly meeting new people, and every so often, we will befriend someone who doesn't respect one or more of our truths—and guess what happens to that person? They are removed from the group. We simply don't have time to deal with the hostility that accompanies disrespect. The thing is, we don't expect anyone to take on our truths. We don't shy away from letting people know what they are, but that's so everyone knows where they stand. However, if you are going to argue with any of us about our belief systems, you've got to go!

One of my long-term goals is to live a stress-free and peaceful life. While I understand that it's impossible to completely eliminate stress from my life, if I can eliminate the thing that's causing me stress, I will do that. I would advise you to take the same approach. Diversity is a wonderful thing; however, if the people you currently associate with won't respect your truth, it's time to find some new friends.

Standing in your truth takes you to a whole new level in your personal development journey. It's something you need to achieve or you will hinder your progress. It's like when snakes shed their skin; this process is called ecdysis, and it happens between four and twelve times per year. A snake's body keeps growing, but its skin doesn't, so the skin sheds and new, roomier skin forms to accommodate the growth. Shedding also gets rid of harmful parasites. What's even more interesting is that just before the shedding takes place, the skin starts turning blue and the snake's eyes get cloudy, which restricts their vision. This is how the snake knows it is time to shed its skin. The snake will then rub its head against something erosive like a stone; this rubbing tears open the outer layer, allowing the snake to free itself from its skin. This process can take a few days or it can take a few weeks, depending on the size of the snake, the condition of its body, and the environment. Once the new skin is revealed, the snake's vision is restored and it is free to continue with its life.

A snake must shed its skin or it will suffer, and the snake knows when the time is right to do so. I doubt it's a very comfortable experience—with blue skin and blurred vision, the snake has to rub its head against something to tear open the skin, and then it has to find its way out of the skin without being able to see properly. Snake owners have said that their pets become very cranky during this period, indicating that shedding their skin is not something they enjoy. To make matters worse, it happens several times a year! Similarly, you will know when it's time to stand in your truth because life will become very uncomfortable. You will despise being fake and surrounding yourself with people who don't really know you. You will have sleepless nights because your spirit won't let you rest about making this transformation. When you do decide to make the change, it won't be an easy one. Like the snake, you will need to isolate yourself and figure it out. You will face a lot of opposition, which will discourage you from continuing the journey. But just like the snake might experience pain during the shedding process and want to give up, it knows it must persevere or it will die. In the same way, you too must persevere with the process or you will never become who you were destined to be.

I believe that when you are building the foundation of your life, you can't afford to enjoy the luxury of balance. You must work extremely hard to build a solid foundation, but once it's built, you can relax a bit and start working on balancing your life. In the final chapter, you will learn how to live in sweet harmony and create balance between your personal life and your career.

CHAPTER 9:

LIVING A BALANCED LIFE: HOW TO SYNCHRONIZE YOUR CAREER AND PERSONAL LIFE

I remember the days when there was no order or structure to my life. Things just happened when they happened, and for a long time, I was okay with that. But once I started my self-development journey, I realized I would never be truly fulfilled if I didn't create balance. Once I had achieved certain milestones, I knew I had to organize my life in a way that allowed me to work on myself, spend time with loved ones, enjoy my hobbies, and write my books. It was challenging because there are so many things pulling at you that's it's easy to lose balance. The problem is that when one thing is out of alignment, everything else crumbles. Nevertheless, through trial and error, I eventually managed to get it right, and I am in a good space right now. In this final chapter, you will learn how to live a balanced life without neglecting the things you love the most.

What Does a Balanced Life Look Like?

I have learned there are eight foundations to a balanced life. When any of these things are out of alignment, I lose balance. It takes an extreme level of discipline to maintain a balanced life because it's all about timing. I hear a lot of people making excuses as to why they can't incorporate certain habits into their lives, but when I evaluate their lives, I see that they waste a lot of time on fruitless activities like watching TV and scrolling through social media. Now, I'm not saying that you can't have downtime—I take two days off per week to chill out and spend time with myself. However, I make sure I get the most important things done first. Here are the eight elements of a balanced life:

1. **Mental Health:** Your mental health should be your priority because the quality of your mind will determine the quality of your life. It is important to maintain a mindset that is resilient, positive, and free from clutter. Activities I have found to improve my mental health include:

   - Reading self-help books

   - Affirmations

   - Meditation

   - Journaling

2. **Physical Health:** A healthy body equals a healthy mind and vice versa. Are you starting to see why it's so important to maintain balance in your life? When your mind is unhealthy, your body suffers, and when your body is unhealthy, your mind suffers. Physical health is about moving your body, consuming a healthy diet, and getting enough sleep. Your body is your temple—you only get one, and

if you don't take care of it, you won't be able to function properly. Activities I have found to improve my physical health include:

- Getting enough sleep. Experts suggests adults should get seven to nine hours of quality sleep per night. However, I have found that six hours' sleep is enough for me. I know this because even if I don't set an alarm, I will wake up after six hours feeling fresh and rejuvenated. Work out how many hours of sleep you need per night and stick to this.

- Ditch processed foods, processed sugar, and soda. Replace the standard American diet with whole foods such as fruits, vegetables, legumes, lean protein, and whole-wheat bread, rice, and pasta.

- Drink at least two liters of water per day.

- Work out for at least thirty minutes per day.

3. **Emotional Health:** Your emotional health is different to your mental health and revolves around understanding the role your thoughts and feelings play in your life. They impact your level of motivation, your actions, and ultimately, your results. Experts refer to this as "emotional intelligence." I would advise that you read Daniel Goleman's book, *Emotional Intelligence: Why It Can Matter More Than IQ* to gain a better understanding of this concept. In the meantime, activities I have found to improve my emotional health include:

- Managing stress effectively
- Practicing mindfulness

- Speaking about your emotions
- Practicing gratitude
- Practicing breathing exercises

4. **Spiritual Health:** Your spiritual health is about the fulfilment you get from connecting with something greater than yourself; seeking purpose, meaning, inner peace, and living according to the morals and values you have set for yourself. It is often assumed that you can only live a spiritual life if you practice a certain religion. This is inaccurate. How you choose to express your spirituality is up to you; it can be through religion, the universe, or nature. Activities that improve your spiritual health include:

- Praying to the god you serve
- Connecting with people who share your spirituality
- Connecting with nature
- Reading spiritual texts and practicing what you read
- Volunteering
- Creating a sacred space in your home

5. **Environmental Health:** Your environment is where you live. Whether you live in shared accommodation or you live alone, your environment should be conducive to success. Living in a messy house has a direct impact on your mental health, and if your mental health is unstable, it will destabilize every area of your life. Activities that improve your environmental health include:

- Decluttering
- Spring-cleaning

- Organizing spaces
- Not leaving dishes in the sink
- Cleaning a little bit each day
- Establishing a regular cleaning schedule
- Buying efficient cleaning tools

6. **Social Health:** Spending time with friends, family, and loved ones is important. But it is also important that your relationships are healthy. Surround yourself with positive, supportive people who want the best for you. Activities to improve your social health include:

   - Schedule time to spend with your loved ones.
   - Evaluate your relationships and eliminate those that are not serving you.
   - Work on your communication skills to improve your interactions with your loved ones.

7. **Financial Health:** One of the major stressors in life is finances. Research suggests that seventy-eight percent of the American population live paycheck to paycheck. Twenty-seven percent of United States adults don't have any emergency savings, and seventy-seven percent of American households are in debt. If you want to live your best life, sorting out your finances is a must. Here are some activities to improve your financial health:

   - Maintain a budget.
   - Save for a rainy day.
   - Have a side hustle.
   - Pay off credit cards on time.

8. **Occupational Health:** Another major problem people have is that they hate their jobs. You will never live a fulfilling life if you hate your job. If you dislike your job, it is important you find a career that means something to you. Here are some activities to improve your occupational health:

- Determine what you are passionate about.
- Find a job that aligns with your passions.
- Even if you don't like your current job, do something every day that fulfils you.
- Develop your skills so you can find a new job.
- If your goal is to become self-employed, work on that.

How to Incorporate These Eight Elements Into Your Life

Living a balanced life can be simple if you are willing to make the required sacrifices. As mentioned, it takes an extreme level of discipline, but if you are able to keep a schedule and say no to the things that don't serve you, you will achieve your goal to live a balanced life.

Keep a Schedule: Scheduling your time will make it a lot easier to live a balanced life. It's impossible to maintain balance if you are spending too much time on one thing. With a schedule, you assign time to the things you want to do. Note that this isn't a one-and-done schedule, because things change. I have blocked out times for the eight foundations—they don't change unless something really important comes up. But sometimes, you might need to make a weekly schedule to accommodate other events such as doctors' appointments, a friend's birthday, or a wedding anniversary. Here are some tips on how to create a schedule:

- As mentioned, the eight foundations should be blocked in as part of your daily routine. For example, working on my physical, mental, and emotional health are all things I do in the morning.

- Pencil in the hours you work per week.

- Pencil in the time you will spend on your hobbies.

- Pencil in the time you will spend with your family.

- Pencil in the time you will spend with your friends.

- You will usually know in advance if anything else needs to be added to your schedule, so pencil those things in as they come up.

- Be sure to assign the amount of time you will spend on each activity. For example, two hours having dinner with Sarah.

Say No: The universe has a funny way of testing you to see if you are serious about the things you say you want out of life. Once you decide to navigate this balancing act, the entire world will start demanding your time. You will experience things like your boss asking you to work overtime so you can help out on a project, your sister needing you for something, your cousin needing you for something, your parents needing you for something. The list will be endless. But you will also notice that the things people need you for are not important; it won't be the end of the world if you don't help them—but they will try and make out like it will be. Unless you are dealing with a life-or-death situation, say no to anything that interrupts your schedule.

Living a balanced life is extremely fulfilling, but I also understand that it's a lot to take in. When I started reading about this, I thought it was going to be impossible. But the key is to work on one foundation at a time; don't try and do everything at once or you will overwhelm yourself and get burned-out. After you have mastered one element, move on to the next. Remember, self-discipline is your best friend. On the days that you don't feel like doing it, do it anyway. But when you do fail, don't beat yourself up about it—just keep trying, and eventually, you will reach your destination.

CONCLUSION

I f you're reading this page because you've read every single page that came before it, I want to congratulate you, and I want you to give yourself a pat on the back. Why? Because according to the American Reading Habits Survey, in one year, only forty-eight percent of adults finished reading an entire book. What I took from this statistic is that if you don't have the discipline to finish reading one book, you won't have the discipline to change your life—because that's what it's going to take: a whole lot of self-discipline.

Listen: execution is the key to success! Let me say it again for the people at the back: execution is the key to success! Without doing the work, nothing happens. And that's the hard part, doing the work. I had a lot of fun writing out my goals, creating vision boards, and doing all the other things I needed to do to prepare myself for success, but when it came time to do the work, procrastination kicked my behind in a major way. As much as I wanted to turn my dreams into reality, the bad habits I had developed over the years hijacked my drive and I found it extremely difficult to get stuff done. But I kept trying, and eventually, I turned things around. Do you remember that quote, "A journey of a thousand miles begins with a single step"? Well, who takes a thousand-mile journey and doesn't encounter obstacles and need to take breaks? There were days when I just had to get back into bed, put the covers over my head and resign myself to defeat. Those days were my pit stops on my journey. When I faced an obstacle, I found my way around it, but in most cases, it took me a while to figure out how to overcome the obstacle. Trust me when I tell you that you will get there if you don't give up.

Think about it like this. Let's say you have a large tree in your garden that needs to be cut down. You know a little bit about cutting down trees, but you're not an expert. So, you get your axe and start hacking away at the tree. The axe is small, and the tree is huge. There is no way on Earth you are going to chop that tree down in one sitting. So, day after day, you return to the tree and hack. To begin with, it doesn't look like you're making any progress, but as the weeks and the months of your daily hacking go by, the tree falls. Had you given up because you couldn't see any progress, the tree would still be standing tall, wreaking havoc in your garden.

Your goals are the same as the tree—they are large and intimidating because all you've got is a little bit of willpower, and you are not confident that you'll achieve them. But if you keep hacking at your dreams day after day, you will start seeing progress and eventually, you will be able to tick that goal off your list.

The choice is yours. No one can do this for you. I wish I could tell you that this is going to be easy, but I would be lying. It will be *easier* because I've given you a blueprint to follow, but it definitely will not be easy.

I also want to remind you that success is a lifestyle and not a onetime event. Aim to make achieving your goals your new normal. Every year, you should be working towards something new. Aspire to continuously become a better version of yourself so you never have any regrets.

I wish you every success on your journey to becoming a remarkable woman!

THANKS FOR READING!

I really hope you enjoyed this book and, most of all, got more value from it than you had to give.

It would mean a lot to me if you left an Amazon review—I will reply to all questions asked!

Simply find this book on Amazon, scroll to the reviews section, and click "Write a customer review".

Or Scan the QR Code on Your Phone:

Be sure to check out my email list, where I am constantly adding tons of value. The best way to get on the list currently is by visiting https://pristinepublish.com/empathbonus and entering your email.

Here, I'll provide actionable information that aims to improve your enjoyment of life. I'll update you on my latest books, and I'll even send free e-books that I think you'll find useful.

Kindest regards,

Judy Dyer

ALSO BY
Judy Dyer

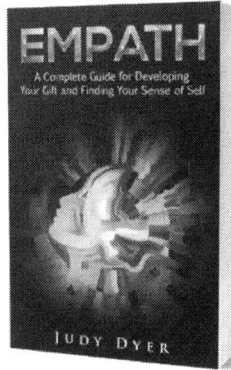

Grasp a better understanding of your gift and how you can embrace every part of it so your life is enriched day by day.

Visit: www.pristinepublish.com/judy

Or Scan the QR Code on Your Phone:

REFERENCES

Abrams, Z. (2023). *The science of why friendships keep us healthy.* American Psychological Association.

Allen, S. (2018). *The Science of Generosity.*

Backlinko Team (2024). *Revealing Average Screen Time Statistics for 2024.*

Barson, M. (2019). Steven Spielberg | Biography, Movies, & Facts. In: *Encyclopædia Britannica.*

Batdorf, E. (2024). *Majority of Americans Live Paycheck To Paycheck – Forbes Advisor.*

Berman, R. (2022). *Longevity: Having a purpose may help you live longer, healthier.*

Botsman, R. (2023). *'Procrastination is the thief of time'.*

Brower, T. (2023). Purpose May Be The Key To Happiness: 3 Reasons Why. *Forbes.*

Calm Blog. (n.d.). *How to be more resilient: 8 ways to build your resilience.*

Cherry, K. (2019). *Why Freud's Pleasure Principle Motivate Behaviors.* Verywell Mind.

Cherry, K. (2022). *Locus of control and your life.* Verywell Mind.

Cherry, K. (2022). *What Is Parkinson's Law?* Verywell Mind.

Clarisse (2019). *Why 85% of People Hate their Jobs.* Staff Squared.

Clear, J. (2018). *Atomic habits: the life-changing million-copy #1 bestseller.* Random House.

Crockett, L. (2012). *How to have self-confidence: Building self-esteem one thought, one word at a time.* CreateSpace Independent Pub.

Cuncic, A. (2022). *Imposter Syndrome: Why You May Feel Like a Fraud.* Verywell Mind.

Davis, J. (2022). *15 classic fashion pieces every woman should own.* Harper's BAZAAR.

Deane, M. (2022). *Top 6 Reasons New Businesses Fail.* Investopedia.

Degges-White, S., & Van Tieghem, J. P. (2015). *Toxic friendships: Knowing the Rules and Dealing with the Friends Who Break Them.* Rowman & Littlefield.

Dennish, A. (2018). *Acceptance – Anne Dennish – Writer/Author.*

www.dundee.ac.uk. (n.d.). *Links between confidence and mental health laid bare | University of Dundee, UK.*

Dweck, C.S. and Yeager, D.S. (2019). Mindsets: A View From Two Eras. *Perspectives on Psychological Science,* 14(3), pp.481–496.

ET Online (2023). *'Embrace what you don't know.' Bill Gates shares 5 things he never got to hear at his college graduation.* The Economic Times.

FOX (2024). *More than 1 in 4 US adults have no emergency savings, survey finds.* LiveNOW from FOX | Breaking News, Live Events.

Gilliard, J. M. (2016). *The Little Book About Toxic Friends: How to Recognize a Toxic Relationship.* Xlibris Corporation.

Grotberg, E. H. (2001). *Tapping Your Inner Strength: How to Find the Resilience to Deal with Anything.* New Age Books

Hill, N. (2016). *Think and Grow Rich: The Classic Edition: The All-Time Masterpiece on Unlocking Your Potential—In Its Original* 1937 Edition. Penguin.

Jacobs, R. (2017). *The 7 Questions to Find Your Purpose.* Watkins Media Limited.

Jayagopi, D.B., Hung, H., Yeo, C. and Gatica-Perez, D. (2009). Modeling Dominance in Group Conversations Using Nonverbal Activity Cues. *IEEE Transactions on Audio, Speech, and Language Processing*, 17(3), pp.501–513.

Jennings, J. (2012). *Give Me Confidence: 10 Powerful Ways to Rapidly Build Your Self-Confidence Today.* Createspace Independent Pub.

Jensen, K. (2022). *Over 50% of Adults Have Not Finished a Book in the Last Year.* BOOK RIOT.

Kaufman, S.B. and Jauk, E. (2020). Healthy Selfishness and Pathological Altruism: Measuring Two Paradoxical Forms of Selfishness. *Frontiers in Psychology*, 11(1006).

Kennedy, S. (2017). *The Power of Putting Yourself First: A Guide to Becoming the Best Version of You Ever.* Kennedy Media and Entertainment Publishing.

King University (2019). *The link between social media and body image.* King University Online.

Kripalu.org. (2024).

Laysears-Smith, R. R. (2013). *Thoughts that Feed the Resilient Mind.* Balboa Press.

Lee, B.Y. (2024). Study Finds Less Loneliness Among Those With A Sense Of Purpose. *Forbes.*

Levin, N. (2019). *Permission to Put Yourself First: Questions, Exercises, and Advice to Transform All Your Relationships.* Hay House, Inc.

Li, S., Hughes, J.L. and Myat Thu, S. (2014). The Links Between Parenting Styles and Imposter Phenomenon. *Psi Chi Journal of Psychological Research*, 19(2), pp.50–57.

Loncar, T. (2021). *A Decade of Power posing: Where Do We stand?* BPS.

MacInnes, P. (2008). *Beyoncé? We think you mean Sasha Fierce.* the Guardian.

Mesibov, G. (2004). *Outer Strength, Inner Strength.* Xulon Press.

Messiah, L. (2018). *Dressing Your Body Type*

Muschett, S.E. (2021). *Cultivating a Resilient Mind: A Guide To Fighting Trauma In A Post Pandemic Society.* Independently Published.

Nandy, D. (2023). *The Complete Guide to Living a Balanced Lifestyle.* Independently Published.

National Institutes of Health (NIH). (2015). *Human Brain Appears 'Hard-Wired' for Hierarchy.*

Newsroom.accenture.com. (n.d.). *Accenture Research Finds Listening More Difficult in Today's Digital Workplace.*

O'Brien, D., Main, A., Kounkel, S. and Stephan, A.R. (2019). *Purpose Is Everything.* Deloitte Insights.

Palmer, P. J. (2015). *Let Your Life Speak: Listening for the Voice of Vocation.* John Wiley & Sons.

www.piedmont.org. (n.d.). *4 reasons friends and family are good for your health.*

Prosper. (n.d.). *Journaling to increase self-awareness.*

Ramsey Solutions (2021). *Average American Debt.* Ramsey Solutions.

Ravikant, K. (2013). *Live Your Truth.* Founderzen.

Roberts, T.J. (2023). *Top 3 Reasons for Divorce.* Terry & Roberts.

Rockefeller, J. D. (2017). *How to Set and Achieve Goals.* The Publisher, LLC.

Rout, S. (2015). *Live your Balanced Life Now: A Guide to Finding True Balance, Enjoying More Time and Living a Life of Abundance, Pure Joy and Love.* CreateSpace Independent Pub.

Sander, L. (2019). *What does clutter do to your brain and body?* NewsGP.

Schwantes, M. (2016). *Science Says 92 Percent of People Don't Achieve Their Goals. Here's How the Other 8 Percent Do.* Inc.com.

Smiley, R. (2017). *Stand by Your Truth.* Simon and Schuster.

Stevenson, B. and Wolfers, J. (2009). The Paradox of Declining Female Happiness. *Federal Reserve Bank of San Francisco, Working Paper Series*, pp.1.00048.000.

Suttie, J. (2021). *Does Venting Your Feelings Actually Help?* Greater Good.

Sylvester Stallone | Biography, Movies, & Facts. (2019). In: *Encyclopædia Britannica*.

Teach Different. (n.d.). *'Out of suffering have emerged the strongest souls; the most massive characters are seared with scars.' Kahlil Gibran - Suffering*.

The Decision Lab. (n.d.). *Law of the instrument*.

The University of Texas Permian Basin | UTPB. (2020). *How Much of Communication Is Nonverbal? | UT Permian Basin Online*.

Thibodeaux, W. (2016). *What a Lack of Eye Contact Says About You, According to Science (and How to Fix It)*. [online] Inc.com.

Thompson, B.S. and H. (2013). *Now Hear This! Most People Stink at Listening [Excerpt]*. Scientific American.

Tikkanen, A. (2019). Jim Carrey | Biography, Movies, & Facts. In: *Encyclopædia Britannica*.

WebMD. (n.d.). *The Emotional Shock of Retirement*.

Women's Confidence. (2021). *Women's Confidence*.

Wong, K. (2015). *How to Deal With People Who Undermine Everything You Do*. Lifehacker.

World Health Organization (2019). *Suicide Prevention.* Who.int.

World Health Organization (2024). *Physical activity.* World Health Organization.

Young, V. (2011). *The 5 Types of Impostor Syndrome.* Impostor Syndrome Institute.

Young, V. (2023). *Where Does Impostor Syndrome Come From — and Why It Matters - Impostor Syndrome Institute.* Impostor Syndrome Institute.

Yu, X., Xiong, F., Zhang, H., Ren, Z., Liu, L., Zhang, L. and Zhou, Z. (2023). The Effect of Social Support on Depression among Economically Disadvantaged College Students: The Mediating Role of Psychological Resilience and the Moderating Role of Geography. *International Journal of Environmental Research and Public Health*, 20(4), p.3053.

Printed in Great Britain
by Amazon